"Grace makes beauty out of
Ott writes with openness, passion, and hard-won insight ~
the grace he found in U2 and C. S. Lewis when walking through
one of life's most troubling episodes. Readers will receive the
gifts of Ott's honesty, wisdom, and enthusiasm for life from this
book, as I did, and will find that at the intersection of U2, Lewis,
and scripture, he has built a richly layered playlist.

—SCOTT CALHOUN, Professor of English, Cedarville University,
director of the U2 Conference and editor of *Exploring U2: Is This
Rock 'n' Roll? Essays on the Music, Work, and Influence of U2*

U2 and C. S. Lewis! What an amazing combination that guides
the soul soaked in sorrow into a place of illuminated peace.
Kevin Ott brilliantly takes a deep emotional dive that surfaces
in the presence of Jesus. I am so pleased to recommend this book
to everyone who has known depression, suffering, and sadness.
Kevin artfully combines his skill as a worship leader and inspira-
tional speaker to help us understand the liminal space between
brokenness and healing.

—RANDY PHILLIPS, of the musical group Phillips, Craig & Dean

Kevin writes about music in a way I've never seen before. It
brings all the deeper things of our existence—joy, philosophy,
theology, imagination, and hope—to life. It transforms you.

—MOSES SUMNEY, acclaimed recording artist and songwriter, and
a collaborator with the Grammy-winning artist Beck

Ott's insightful analysis and personal testimonial result in a persuasive and powerful presentation of the ability of artistic expression and spiritual exploration to aid in healing and growth. The author's own training and experience as a musician, composer, songwriter, worship leader, author, blogger, and film critic give him a unique perspective on creativity and the Creator. Readers will discover how it is possible to tap into unexpected depths of joy even while wrestling with profound loss.

—REV. JON EYMANN, MA, Marriage and Family Therapist, Psychotherapist, and Manager of Crisis Services, Santa Barbara County Behavioral Wellness

Kevin's intense hunger for God comes through on every page. This book does more than just bring joy into times of sorrow. It will change your life and awaken a deeper hunger to pursue God with all of your heart.

—DR. KODJOE SUMNEY, Founder of Mission Africa Incorporated, an award-winning humanitarian group in Africa, and the presiding pastor over the Annual Parliamentary Conference, a national prayer conference held in the parliament of Ghana, Africa

SHADOWLANDS

AND SONGS OF LIGHT

AN EPIC JOURNEY INTO JOY AND HEALING

KEVIN OTT

BroadStreet
PUBLISHING

BroadStreet Publishing Group, LLC
Racine, Wisconsin, USA
BroadStreetPublishing.com

SHADOWLANDS AND SONGS OF LIGHT: AN EPIC JOURNEY INTO JOY AND HEALING

ISBN-13: 978-1-4245-5291-7 (hardcover)
ISBN-13: 978-1-4245-5292-4 (e-book)

Stock or custom editions of BroadStreet Publishing titles may be purchased in bulk for educational, business, ministry, fundraising, or sales promotional use. For information, please e-mail info@broadstreetpublishing.com.

Cover design by Chris Garborg, garborgdesign.com
Interior design and typeset by Katherine Lloyd, TheDESKonline.com

16 17 18 19 20 5 4 3 2 1

Dedication

For the daring ones who raised me—Mom and Dad, who established me in Christ's words, and then used backpacking in the Sierras, imagination, and unconditional love to show me Christ's heart; my brother Evan, whose contagious love of reading, music, and humor brought constant joy to my childhood; and my brother Ian, who opened C. S. Lewis' world to me in Oxford and inspired me to believe that anything is possible.

I long for melodies

To chase away the darkness of my fears

And tickle me with laughter

– SALLY OTT

CONTENTS

Part IV · Every Breaking Wave: When the Flesh Is Weak

Part V · There Is No End to Love: Further Up and Further In

PART I

WHERE THE STREETS
HAVE NO NAME:
THE ROAD
TO THE SECRET PLACE

Always Winter but Never Christmas

The news came while I held the book *Planet Narnia* in my hands, about to turn the page. My dad was calling from California, three days after Christmas. I was in snowy Ohio, and getting a call from him while I traveled was unusual. Although close, we weren't phone people, instead preferring face-to-face conversations, usually with a good cup of coffee or a leisurely dinner.

There had been several missed calls already and urgent text messages asking me to call back as soon as possible, though I hadn't heard or seen any of them. I had been away from my phone all morning, and I didn't think to check my phone as I sat down to read. I was too eager to dive into the world of Narnia. Another call came in. This time I was within earshot of the phone, and I looked and saw all the missed messages. Fear fluttered in my stomach as I lifted the phone to my ear. Something wasn't right.

By the time the conversation ended, tears slid down my face and fell onto the book.

My mom had passed away during the night.

No one had seen it coming. She had some unusual health

problems for a sixty-two-year-old, but nothing that had brought the "d" word to our lips during our Christmas celebration. Only a week earlier she had called me, excited about watching the Christmas movie *Elf* with me when I returned home.

I had been finishing page twenty-nine of *Planet Narnia* when the call came in. A few weeks later, I returned to the book to distract myself, but as I turned to page thirty, I couldn't bear reading it. The page became a point of terrible demarcation, a boundary line as imposing as the Abyss. A few weeks earlier, when I had read page twenty-nine, my mom had been alive. But on page thirty she was gone from the world. A sliver of paper had formed a chasm as significant as BC and AD in history, and it now divided my life.

My mom loved books like *Planet Narnia*. She would not have approved of me putting it down. But I couldn't help it. Reading about Narnia had changed from joy to dismal darkness. A shadow had fallen over those lands, enshrouding even the golden face of Aslan the great lion. In the story *The Magician's Nephew*, a miraculous fruit from Aslan saved Digory's ailing mother from death. But instead of a lion bringing a gift to me in the nick of time, a season when it is "always winter but never Christmas"[1] came, as if the White Witch had returned and re-established her terrible kingdom.

Moments of bitterness—and envy—struck when I least expected it. The thought of Christians I knew who had received miracles made me angry. Why hadn't God done a miracle for me?

Many of us struggle with the theological problem of pain, asking the age-old question, "Why, God?" The same question troubled C. S. Lewis, who lost his mother and his wife to cancer.

Bono, the lead singer and lyricist of U2, also wrestled with the question; he lost his mother to a brain aneurysm when he was fourteen. It is the struggle of every doubter who asks, "If God is both good and all powerful, why is there suffering?" The Bible has a powerful answer to that question, but the emotional bitterness of the question still aches in the front of our minds like a throbbing headache during difficult times, and especially when we lose someone or something precious to us. And if the sting is severe enough, grief turns into hopelessness.

Of course, the Bible resists such hopelessness, and for good reason. We could spend our lifetimes tracing the stratospheric arc of Christ's triumph over sin, death, and the Devil, and never come to the end of it.

In fact, for a brief time after my mom's death, the power of Christ's triumph roared through my spirit. At her funeral I even sang a song of jubilant praise, rejoicing in her life and in the victory she had found in Christ. I wanted to be strong for my family during that time, and God aided me. Those early days flashed with the light of heaven, a wordless glimpse of what I would later rediscover and place into words.

But as time passed, as the initial shock wore off and the full weight of the loss began to settle in, the light in my heart grew dim and flickered on and off unpredictably, and I wrestled terribly with my mother's passing. Whenever the stormy days hit, none of the trumpet blasts or shouts of Jesus' victory broke through the noise. With a tired shake of my head, I would read, "Brothers and sisters, we do not want you to be uninformed about those who sleep in death, so that you do not grieve like the rest of mankind, who have no hope" (1 Thess. 4:13 NIV), and "Where, O death, is your victory? Where, O death, is your sting?" (1 Cor. 15:55 NIV).

On the darkest days, such passages would mock me. "Where, O death, is your sting?" the verse would say, and I would bitterly reply, "It's right here in my chest!"

Questions haunted me. How is a Christian's grief different *experientially* from the world's grief? Yes, we have hope about life after death, but what do we do with it? Is it just an intellectual proposition that we store away with our memory verses? If it is supposed to change the way we grieve, how does that happen? How does it travel from abstract head knowledge to concrete, rib-shaking reality?

A cold, tired flatness settled over me as I sought answers. I tried to write a book that compared Lewis' *The Problem of Pain* with the works of Beethoven, but there was no fire in it. Lewis' words—at times carried along in *The Problem of Pain* with the diplomatic candor of a doctor explaining a disease—felt dry and lifeless to me, which was unusual. Equally strange, Beethoven's wondrous music fell flat. I had no real joy in sight.

Then September 9, 2014 came. I did not know it at the time, but that day—which began rather strangely—would change the course of my life. That morning, I was hiking on local beach trails when my brother texted me that U2 had just released their new album, *Songs Of Innocence*, for free on iTunes. A lifelong U2 fan, I came close to leaping and shouting in celebration right there on the dusty sea cliff trails. It was a windy day, and the coastal environment seemed to rejoice with me. The ice plants and coastal sage scrub shivered with goose bumps as Bono sang about miracles and California sunsets, and the Santa Barbara surf clapped to the music with every breaking wave.

The album awakened something deep within me. I rushed home and poured my thoughts into a review of the album. A few days later, Scott Calhoun, an author and scholar (and a die-hard U2 fan like myself), read my review online and contacted me. As we spoke, he mentioned bringing U2 and C. S. Lewis together in a book.

Another light turned on. What if I wrote about my experiences with U2's music instead of Beethoven's? (Sorry, Ludwig.) The task of capturing such personal moments, however, felt daunting. God had used piles of U2 albums in my life, but I had never tried to shape those experiences into a book. Such experiences were intensely personal and difficult to articulate, and I had been stuck in exhaustion and mire. The cold flatness wouldn't leave. I doubted myself.

But as I placed the books of C. S. Lewis and the music of U2 into dialogue—with Christ facilitating between the two parties—God cut through the difficulty and began to address my questions about grief. He threw the gates open, and his answers astonished me.

The ice inside began to melt. Something in U2's music violently but gloriously cracked open the revelations that Lewis had placed with such care in his books—especially his idea of Joy. Soon my feet were walking along a path again. I was on a journey, and it was transforming me from the inside out.

I should clarify something here: I'm not interested in placing Lewis or U2 on infallible pedestals. I don't necessarily agree with every word they've said from the stage, sung in a studio, or written in a book. But during a period of great inner darkness, the words of Lewis and the musical ideas of U2 became "right Jerusalem blades"[2] in the nimble hands of the Holy Spirit. He cut straight through the thick of night.

The answers led me into what I now call the Stages of Joy. These Stages form an adventurer's map, containing all the things that Lewis and U2 have written about in their work: grand quests, larger-than-life worlds, roaring lions, ancient villains, soaring anthems, songs of heartache, and truth hidden away beneath the garbage and mean streets of this world that Lewis dubbed the "weeping valley."[3]

But this book is not just for those who have lost a loved one. Death has many kin, and they come in many forms, not just funerals. When anything precious comes to an unwanted end, whether it's a relationship, a career, a ministry, or our health, grief speckles us with its shadows.

In this journey, with the help of a large stack of C. S. Lewis books, we will steal down the shadowy slopes and switchback trails together to explore the weeping valley. Along the way, we will unearth many of the most effective (and affecting) musical structures behind U2 songs, and I will provide a U2 playlist that I've curated and carefully tied to each chapter. (The playlist will begin in chapter 2, after we've explored C. S. Lewis' unusual concept of Joy in chapter 1.)

Together we will go on a quest for Joy. And when we are done, you'll be able to listen to each Stage of Joy—a musical meditation to help you remember the points of the book for years to come by simply pushing *play*.

CHAPTER 1

HEAVEN IS ON THE MOVE: STABS OF LONGING

What a long night on the mountain—one that allowed little sleep. We had pitched our tent on the summit, and the wind beat on us until dawn, whipping the tent's walls like flags. I was in grade school at the time, and the fierce blowing unnerved me. But my mother, an adventurous woman who had earned the nickname "Mountain Mama" for her love of backpacking, thought the predicament—the wind and freezing darkness surrounding our tent on a mountain—was paradise itself.

As dawn broke, the wind weakened. I emerged from our battered shelter and stepped to the mountain's edge. A sunrise that seemed as large as the universe opened the morning like a Christmas present, its light glittering across the surface of the rivers and lakes below—silver bows and blue ribbons. I could see miles in every direction, with the mountainous green national parks to the west and the red dust deserts of Nevada to the east.

The sight reminded me of an album cover that bore four musicians standing near a praying cactus tree in a cinematic panorama. I would learn later that the deserts in the distance were not far from where U2 staged the photo shoots for their album *The Joshua Tree*.[1]

After a few moments of standing there, I heard a roar above. As I looked up, an F-4 Phantom fighter plane streaked across the sky, flying low over the mountain's summit. The jet flew at a slow-enough speed that we could see the pilot as it passed by, and he gave us a thumbs-up.

Something pooled in my heart, an expansive longing that surprised me with its intensity. It was not the desire to see another dawn or fighter jet. Those things were pinpricks that spilled an unexpected blood, a yearning that flowed toward something I could not name. The sensation itself—the sudden yearning for something far off and unknown—was more wonderful than a thousand sunrises and fighter jets.

Later in my adulthood, the longing came again during a lightning storm that I witnessed from the window of an airliner. We were flying above the clouds at night and could see flashes of lightning below us. Above the storm the night was clear, as pristine as a summer evening. The Archer constellation—the centaur warrior who bends his bow back to shoot—glittered above the clouds. As his constellation hovered above the lightning, the sensation again welled up, bringing an overwhelming yearning for something far off. I was almost ecstatic. When the yearning ebbed away, I wanted to feel it again; I longed for the longing.

I had experienced the same feeling when I was a child too. My mom was riding a horse in Montana in Paradise Valley, and I was small enough that I could fit on the saddle in front of her. She gave me M&Ms, one at a time, every few seconds, as we trotted through the wilderness. The candy and my mother's presence brought comfort.

But then another sensation followed. The hugeness of the horse, its head looming before me and towering over my toddler frame, brought the yearning, though it was a quieter kind, filled with the helium of childhood.

I shouldn't be surprised that this longing baptized me again when I visited Oxford, England, where C. S. Lewis had lived and worked for most of his life. I was a high school student and had gone to visit my brother Ian, who was studying at Oxford University. One night while walking across one of the ancient stone bridges—one that Galileo had likely strode across centuries ago—I looked up and saw the constellation Orion glittering like a cross in the sky. At that moment, my brother saw a homeless man huddled in blankets. He opened his grocery bag, pulled out a bottle of vitamins, and gave it to the man.

What an unexpected one-two punch. I saw the heavens glittering in the sky, and then I saw heaven appearing on earth as my brother showed the love of Christ to a stranger. All of it induced something beyond this world, an inconsolable longing that struck me in the streets where Lewis had walked.

C. S. Lewis would have called these moments of longing "stabs of Joy."[2] In my conversations, so few people have heard about Lewis' definition of Joy that when they hear me say the word, they think I'm referring to happiness or pleasure. But this special kind of Joy has little to do with circumstantial happiness. In fact, instead of saying "Stabs of Joy," I find that the term "Stabs of Longing" makes Lewis' meaning more evident to those not familiar with his writings.

These Stabs of Longing feel close to the intense sensations of homesickness—the pangs that come when we see a place from our childhood or hear an old song that's tied to our past. Yet it's not quite nostalgia. It goes beyond that. When this strange Longing stabs us, we feel homesick for a home we've never had.

Dr. Timothy Keller, in one of his sermons at Redeemer Presbyterian Church, talked about this Joy, and he wondered if some faint memory of Eden's paradise—that perfect bliss of fellowship we once enjoyed with God, heart-to-heart and knee-to-knee, sitting with him on top of the world with our feet dangling off the edge—somehow still haunts us.

In his autobiography, *Surprised by Joy: The Shape of My Early Life*, Lewis defined this special kind of Joy as "an unsatisfied desire which is itself more desirable than any other satisfaction."[3] For him, the sensations would strike like lightning bolts. They would flash and then disappear: "Before I knew what I desired, the desire itself was gone, the whole glimpse withdrawn, the world turned commonplace again, or only stirred by a longing for the longing that had just ceased."[4]

While reading a line from Henry Wadsworth Longfellow's *Saga of King Olaf*, the Longing stabbed Lewis, and he described it this way: "Instantly I was uplifted into huge regions of northern sky, I desired with almost sickening intensity something never to be described (except that it is cold, spacious, severe, pale, and remote) and then, as in other examples, found myself at the very same moment already falling out of that desire and wishing I were back in it."[5]

Those few seconds of Longing, at least the ones that Lewis recorded, probably added up to less than a minute on the clock, yet they changed him forever, as he noted: "the reader who finds these three episodes of no interest need read this book no further, for in a sense the central story of my life is about nothing else."[6]

After I lost my mom, I was shocked to discover—especially during the first few weeks after her funeral—these same Stabs of Longing, though in a slightly different form, hiding in the shadows of grief. These pangs shuddered through my spirit with surprising strength and lingered longer than the usual flashes of Joy. I began to question the whole nature of grief. I felt like a man who sits in darkness thinking he is in a prison cell behind locked doors, but when the lights come on he discovers he's free. There is no prison. In fact, he's been sitting in a palace all along.

That's almost how Lewis describes his experience with grief when, at one point in his mourning, the sudden weight of heaven's reality invaded:

One moment last night can be described in similes; otherwise it won't go into language at all. Imagine a man in total darkness. He thinks he is in a cellar or dungeon. Then there comes a sound. He thinks it might be a sound from far off-waves or wind-blown trees or cattle half a mile away. And if so, it proves he's not in a cellar, but free, in the open air. Or it may be a much smaller sound close at hand—a chuckle of laughter. And if so, there is a friend just beside him in the dark. Either way, a good, good sound. I'm not mad enough to take such an experience as evidence for anything. It is simply the leaping into imaginative activity of an idea which I would always have theoretically admitted—the idea that I, or any mortal at any time, may be utterly mistaken as to the situation he is really in.[7]

The pain of losing such a precious treasure removed a veil from my eyes. The facade of this world's so-called ultimate reality became more evident. The skin of the universe was growing thinner and the walls of heaven were growing thicker.

What was really strange, however, was that this presence of Joy did not weaken the strength of grief. In fact, even as Joy came, a house of sorrow was rising over my head.

The House of Grief

In *Surprised by Joy*, C. S. Lewis had the luxury of looking back on his Stabs of Longing like a man watching a train from a platform. The roaring blur of the train excites the man's senses briefly, but then it vanishes and he has all the time he needs to reflect on the train's passing as he stands on the quiet, unmoving platform.

Likewise, in *The Problem of Pain*, Lewis observed human suffering and untied its theological knots from the safe distance of paper, ink, and contemplation.

But when grief hit him the hardest—after he lost his wife to cancer—he recorded sorrow not as a man standing on the platform making quiet observations but as a man snatched up against his will onto the train, trying desperately to keep his hat on. Nothing remained still. His inner world lurched and rattled, and he scribbled his raw, wild observations about grief when the pain was still white-hot. These real-time field reports became the book *A Grief Observed*.

In *A Grief Observed*, the reader gets a sense of unexpected enormity, as if Lewis had stumbled into a giant labyrinth that he had underestimated; and, like any wise explorer who encounters an imposing structure, he looks at it with something akin to fear. The first sentences of *A Grief Observed* capture the moment perfectly: "No one ever told me that grief feels so like fear. I am not afraid, but the sensation is like being afraid. The same fluttering of stomach, the same restlessness, the yawning. I keep on swallowing."[8]

A Grief Observed also feels labor-intensive, exhausted, as if Lewis is dragging himself up the side of the mountain as he writes—a sharp contrast to his previous books. In *Surprised by Joy*, the tone is lighter. Every word springs with energy and moves forward with delight, as if he were strolling through his favorite hills outside Belfast.

In a similar way, Joy—that sharp, wonderful Stab of Longing—has a lithe, muscular lightness to it. It's deft. It produces longing that weighs heavy on the heart, but it does so with precision and coordination—a mix of strength and poise, like the steel toes of a ballerina. There's a glorious drama in it, and Joy strikes with all of it at once. It dashes in with the agility of a hummingbird claiming its nectar from the flower, and then zips away. It pricks, then vanishes, leaving a wake of mystery and longing behind it.

But grief couldn't be more different. It comes, and then it never leaves. It's clumsy and uncoordinated. There's nothing virtuosic about it. It has all the delightful precision of a concussion grenade.

After the initial shock, and after it diffuses over months and years, grief can take a different form. A nurturing melancholy can fill it at times. It hovers and broods over us, like the bright star going about its unwavering, methodical "priestlike task," as the poet Keats wrote.[9] A priest serves others, washes their feet, and removes debris from the spiritual road. Grief, at times, washes our feet too, and it clears a path for Joy. That path, however, also carries with it an unavoidable solitude.

The moment when grief encloses you like a cocoon, you leave this present world. In a sense, you enter a private universe, even as you go about your daily errands. No matter how many bereavement cards or casseroles arrive at your door, no matter how many times someone sits down with you and shares your tears with a reassuring arm around your shoulder, eventually that person will have to leave and return to the affairs of his or her life. No one can enter that place of grief inside your soul and reside there, tasting it day and night, as you must do. The whole experience becomes a quarantine room—a large, empty house that only you can enter. And like a solidly built fortress, it is not going anywhere.

Racing Through a Mansion of Many Rooms, a Nest of Gardens

But the House of Grief is not a one-room apartment where you sit staring at a wall, never to move again. It's not that kind of private universe. It's not a closet. Not a static experience. Once you step inside, you're in perpetual motion. An unseen hand pulls you down new halls, into unfamiliar rooms, a sudden right turn into a courtyard you've never seen before and then a quick left into a ballroom that you didn't know even existed in the house. Something, or *Someone*, is pulling you further into a many-walled nest of gardens within gardens—a mansion with many rooms that lead to a mysterious location deep within.

In other words, grief has linear motion. Progress. A forward leaning. A pilgrim's steady walk. Lewis described it this way:

> Grief is like a long valley, a winding valley where any bend may reveal a totally new landscape. . . . Sometimes the surprise is an opposite one; you are presented with exactly the same sort of country you thought you had left behind miles ago. That is when you wonder whether the valley isn't a circular trench. But it isn't. There are partial recurrences, but the sequence doesn't repeat.[10]

Grief's strange, slightly familiar but different terrain can feel horrifying at times—more like a scary house of mirrors than a mansion. But even when terror and confusion abound, there is still motion. There is direction, and a purpose behind the motion. Lewis makes a profound discovery: grief is not cyclical. It's not like the clinical routine of an annual medical exam. It's a long journey along a linear path that never sees the same landscape twice.

It's a quest story.

You're a traveler in a strange land, you feel a drive toward a destination (though you don't know its name yet), and every turn of the road brings you to a blank edge of the map. Joy and its Stabs of Longing have this quest-like motion too. Joy drove Lewis to search for truth, and the insatiable pursuit culminated in his faith. In his own words regarding that Longing, "the central story of my life is about nothing else."[11]

Now we have common ground: Joy and grief both produce intense linear motion toward a destination, though we do not yet know the destination.

And it is this shared motion that begins the Stages of Joy.

Scripture

"Rise, let us be going" (Matt. 26:46).

Notes for the Quest

In C. S. Lewis' journey to Christ, the intense longing of Joy caused him to rise and go and hunger and thirst for something greater—something far off on the horizon. The longing stirred him to move. Grief and Joy produce a special kind of motion. And in God's hands, that motion can lead us on a life-changing journey—but only if we're willing to rise from where we lie. Sometimes Jesus' commands are short and simple: "Rise, let us be going." We would do well to obey and take action, even if that action is as simple as getting up from where we lie and moving forward, allowing the linear motion of longing, whether that longing comes from Joy or grief, to draw us down the road on a new journey.

A Prayer for the Journey

Abba Father, stir my heart to rise from complacency or spiritual paralysis—anything that might keep me from setting out on this new road. Help me to recognize and remember the Stabs of

Joy that you've allowed to pierce my life over the years, and help me to recognize Joy when it bids me to "rise, let us be going" during times of great sorrow. In Jesus' name, amen.

More Bible Verses for the Road

Psalm 63

CHAPTER 2

HOMESICK FOR THE STREETS WITH NO NAME: DEEP LONGING

Let us spend what is left in seeking the unpeopled world behind the sunrise.
– *C. S. Lewis*, The Voyage of the Dawn Treader: The Chronicles of Narnia

Song to cue: "Where The Streets Have No Name" from the album *The Joshua Tree*

Inconsolable motion.

If I were to sum up the band U2—every song, every album, and every tour of their almost-forty-year career—those two words would be sufficient.

Inconsolable motion.

It's the motion of something that refuses—obstinately, passionately, religiously—to be comforted or lulled into slowing or stopping. It refuses to settle, and fears self-contentment. It's always straining to see what's beyond the horizon. Its eyes are "impregnated with distance."[1]

Other words such as *restless* or *driven* might apply to U2, but they're not strong enough. The word *inconsolable* expresses the idea of grief at full strength, the most intense state of sorrow in the human experience.[2] The stakes of this word are matters of life and death—the highest stakes.

U2 has always been about the highest stakes: analyzing them, grappling with them, swallowing the emotions that flow from them, and regurgitating their efforts into recorded sound. As *Billboard* once observed: "The foursome had always been earnest and strident—willing to spout off on huge issues like God, death, and war."[3]

Their gutsy, stubborn, almost insane career moves provide plenty of examples of this, whether it was reinventing themselves in 1991 with the revolutionary, experimental masterpiece that no one saw coming—*Achtung Baby*—or giving away their album *Songs Of Innocence* to 500 million iTunes users in 2014.[4]

Inconsolable motion burns in their music too—a desperate hunger for rhythm and racing pulses. And with almost forty years of album reviews written about U2, plenty of people have taken note of this.

The earliest reviews between 1980 and 1982 noted it immediately, especially in The Edge (the nickname for the band's guitarist) and his sprinting, frantic showers of notes: "The Edge's guitar swarms all the way through 'Electric Co.,' almost toppling the song over"[5]; and the "chiming guitar opening [of 'Gloria'] was utterly exhilarating."[6]

In U2's third album, *War*, the critics marveled how "the hurtling ardor of singer and guitarist going at it full-tilt on 'Like A Song'...threatens to spill over into the thunderous rumble of Larry Mullen's drumming...its reverberations set off a chain reaction."[7]

1984's *Unforgettable Fire* provoked this observation: "it radiates wanderlust and love of motion"[8]; and when 1987's *The Joshua Tree* was released, the year that U2 landed on *Time* magazine's cover as "Rock's Hottest Ticket," *Rolling Stone* made note of *The Joshua Tree* and the "driving pulse of Adam Clayton's bass and Larry Mullen Jr.'s drums and the careening wail of the Edge's guitar."[9] From the same era, *Rattle And Hum's* monumental hit "Desire" was described as "intoxicating with a Bo Diddly beat."[10]

In 1991, on *Achtung Baby*, The Edge "uses his guitar as a rhythm instrument...that drives the beat" with "grinding riffs that bounce off Adam Clayton's thick bass line and echo and embellish Larry Mullen Jr.'s drumming."[11]

In 1993, on *Zooropa*, the second installment of their heady trash-pop trilogy, the band provoked this memorable description of the album's opening track: "a stately piano figure, beautiful and foreboding, underlies indecipherable, static-stricken signals from the information-age inferno of Zoo TV. That alluring sonic chaos ultimately yields to the wah-wah blast of the Edge's guitar and the insistent groove of Adam Clayton's bass and Larry Mullen Jr.'s drums."[12]

U2's inconsolable motion wasn't limited to the way they played their instruments. It eventually wandered into their songwriting and their restless splicing of genres. 1997's *Pop* became the clearest example, as this reviewer described: "By now the group has absorbed almost all the history of popular music into its bloodstream, to the extent that their reference points range from cutting-edge techno to old-time country—from The Dust

Brothers to The Louvin Brothers—often within the compass of a single track. Elvis Presley has still not left their building, The Beatles can't be kept out. A cool breeze brings gospel hymns through the window. A monster funk riff shakes the basement."[13]

In 2000, *All That You Can't Leave Behind* was described as having the "charging-horse feel of U2's youth," and a reviewer resorted to military terms to describe the band's soaring power: "From day one, U2 was a rock constellation—a warplane—and we expected epics."[14]

In 2004's *How To Dismantle An Atomic Bomb*, the band's inconsolable motion had not slowed: "The rhythm section is truly unstoppable," a "pounding sonic boom."[15]

In 2009, their twelfth studio album, *No Line On The Horizon*, had "the shimmer of The Edge's guitar and the iron-horse roll of bassist Adam Clayton and drummer Larry Mullen Jr."[16] Even Bono joins the rhythmic fray in this album with his singing, as the same critic observed how Bono's voice moved "in a text-message cadence and drill sergeant's bark, in 'Unknown Caller.'" Elsewhere, the critic describes the "fevered-staccato guitar," and "Mullen's parade-ground drumming, the last so sharp and hard all the way through that it's difficult to tell how much is him and how much is looping (that is a compliment)."[17]

Even though their thirteenth studio album, *Songs Of Innocence*, took five years to make, which caused many people to wonder what was happening to the band, its release proved that U2 had not abandoned their inconsolable motion. If anything, they had intensified it. *Rolling Stone* described *Songs Of Innocence* as a "propulsive delirium of throaty, striding bass…strident, brooding rhythm...[a] tension of metronome-like groove...a great, chunky guitar riff and a beat like a T. Rex stomp."[18]

None of U2's songs, however, so completely capture the idea of inconsolable motion—especially as it exists in grief and Joy—as the legendary anthem "Where The Streets Have No Name."

Joy and Grief in the Streets

The first sixty-eight seconds of U2's "Where The Streets Have No Name," the opening track from *The Joshua Tree*, preaches one of the most goose-bump-inducing sermons ever heard—and it does it without Bono singing a word. This reviewer from NME agrees:

> I'm going to stick my neck out here. "The Joshua Tree" has the greatest first minute of any album ever. There's that subterranean throb, like the world's best headache, until at last, the sad, stately, noble and doomed organ line breaks the surface, backed by The Edge's most dazzling riff (albeit one he demonstrated on *It Might Get Loud* is actually a toddler-worthy doodle with lashings of delay). It's a slow-burn opener so glorious that every hair on my body stands erect, and I spend the rest of "Where The Streets Have No Name" looking like Chewbacca.[19]

What this reviewer doesn't explain, however, is *how* U2 achieves the greatest album opening ever, even though the music is so simple that a small child could play it. There's something amazing happening here, but to fully appreciate it, a short lesson in the physics of sound, without any technical jargon, is in order.

Imagine yourself snapping a group of rubber bands so that each one makes a twanging sound—some high, some low. When you play a chord on the piano, you're striking a bunch of tightly wound strings and making them vibrate. They're giant rubber bands in a wooden box. The higher-sounding strings vibrate faster than the lower-sounding ones, and the mathematical ratios between the vibrations do some strange things to your brain.

In 2011, researchers discovered that the brain likes ratios of sound wave vibrations that have big fat whole numbers, such as 3:2.[20] The brain hates complex ratios such as 3.1465:7.4833. All of the chords that sound nice to the ear are the ones with simple ratios between the notes. The brain has trouble filtering and retaining data from complex ratios; it's like watching a movie on a fuzzy TV from 1974 instead of on an HDTV flat screen. When a chord brings complex, troublesome ratios to the eardrum, it creates what musicians call dissonance—an unpleasant harmony that makes the brain cringe. When a chord has simple ratios, it is called consonance. It's pleasant sounding.

You would think, then, that good songwriters would write nothing but consonant harmony—all simple ratios, no tension, nothing complex.

But good songwriters don't do that.

Good music has a strange nature. It thrives on tension—well, carefully constructed tension. The songs that really pull our heartstrings have more tension than we realize, and much of that tension happens so fast that we're not consciously aware of it.

The opening of "Where The Streets Have No Name" is the

perfect example. A quiet, warm-toned organ begins the song with thick layers of chords. It enters the soundscape as slow as morning light inching across the desert floor. The organ makes the first chord linger, sort of hang in the air, just as the second chord is played. For a brief moment, the two chords overlap, and the spacious, echoing reverb of the mix intensifies the overlap.

When that happens, the overlapping notes—notes that aren't necessarily meant to harmonize—rub against each other and create all sorts of ratio madness: possibly three complex ratios at once. That's plenty of tension, but almost as soon as the ear begins to feel the tension, the organ ends the overlap and returns to playing one chord. It only teases the ear with dissonance. And unless we're really listening with a trained ear, it passes below our radar.

This phenomenon—spikes of dissonance that flicker, then disappear—is probably responsible for about 90 percent of goose bumps experienced in the history of music. In "Where The Streets Have No Name," the chords at 0:19 and 0:53 have the biggest spikes of dissonance. (And those were probably the spots that made that NME reviewer's hair stand on end like Chewbacca's.)

Another interesting thing about dissonance: it can create a sense of change and motion even when the tempo and rhythm of a song stay the same. In our daily lives, tension does that to us too. When we're stressed, when we're behind on a project and frantically trying to meet a deadline, time seems to pass ten times faster than normal. Dissonance in music does a similar thing. It creates this illusion of increased, intensified motion, even when the drummer has not changed the tempo or the beat.

After the organ teases us with dissonance, The Edge's guitar comes in. But it's playing the easiest chord ratios possible—"toddler-worthy," as the reviewer called them. All consonance. No tension whatsoever. The rhythm of the guitar, a simple picking pattern of shimmering high notes, fixes itself in the sonic space. Its hypnotic repetition creates the illusion of something hovering motionless high above, like the fixed light of a star.

There is some movement, yes; The Edge is playing a lilting cluster of notes that might be compared to a lazy pendulum swing—back and forth, back and forth—but the notes are so consonant and banal that the feeling of something frozen in a loop, of a fixed body, overcomes any sense of motion. It shimmers and sparkles, thanks to the delay effects on The Edge's guitar. It's the twinkle of a single star presiding over a shifting world below.

The result is something unusual. The fixed point of the guitar above becomes a reference point, a contrast to the organ. The organ's slow, quiet waves of dissonance stand out.

This is how U2 created its "slow-burn opener," as the reviewer noted—one of the greatest, if not *the* greatest introduction to a song in modern music history.

But U2 is just getting warmed up. At 1:10, the bass and drums join the guitar and organ. Just before this happens, The Edge stops his hypnotic cyclical pattern. Instead of a lazy pendulum-like swinging motion, he levels the rhythm out into a straight, driving sprint, like a jogger shifting into a hard run. He pushes the harmony away from easy consonance and moves it into some slight dissonance. The guitar is now the driver of motion. The bass and drums match this new rhythm with foot stomping, fist-pumping power that energizes and multiples the momentum in the guitar. The instruments, one by one, build upon each other until they become a racing, crashing wave.

When Bono comes in, however, everything changes again. He steps to the front of the mix, and the band's surge of motion moves behind him. The band becomes a single sound, a fixed point in reference to the moving Bono; they're a backdrop to his melody and lyric. The transformation is now complete: every instrument in the band melds together and becomes one fixed star orbiting high above, and Bono is now the one moving restlessly below it as he journeys like a pilgrim through his melody and lyrics; or perhaps he moves more like a hunter, as *Time* magazine noted: "Bono stalks a song as much as sings it, and the moment he takes the stage there is no doubt what his terms are: unconditional surrender."[21]

And all of it, the roaring wave of sound backing Bono and his restless melody, strains forward with Joy—that inconsolable longing for something nameless, for something beyond the horizon where the streets have no name.

Deep Longing

This idea of movement below a fixed point—the organ moving below a guitar part fixed high above, the traveler walking below the fixed point of a star—helps us unfold the next clue about Joy. The intense Longing that defines Joy doesn't just stab us during the ordinary, happy seasons of life. It also sneaks into our mourning, and ignites motion—though in a much different way than it did in normal life.

When C. S. Lewis used the word "stabs" to describe his idea

of Joy, I always pictured it as the blade of a sword ambushing you when you least expect it, piercing your heart, and drawing that inconsolable longing out of it. And perhaps that's a good description of Joy in the ordinary seasons of life.

As the cares of the world and the gnat-like swarms of the day crowd our lives, heaven has to break through those swarms to get our attention, and it uses this Longing as a surgical knife. Joy's sharp Stabs cut through our earthly cares and surprise us. The Holy Spirit sends the Stabs as if he were sending messenger birds—or messenger hummingbirds, to be exact, because of the agile speed of these Stabs that prick and then retreat.

But in the seasons of great sorrow, something strange happens: Joy, for the most part, changes its nature (though there are always exceptions to the rule). It ceases its aggressive incursions. It's no longer a hummingbird darting into our field of vision to distract us from the daily cares, and then fleeing. It doesn't need to. After we have lost someone or something precious in life, the pain has a way of obliterating earthly cares—or, at the very least, weakening those cares. Lewis described it this way:

And no one ever told me about the laziness of grief. Except at my job—where the machine seems to run on much as usual—I loathe the slightest effort. Not only writing but even reading a letter is too much. Even shaving. What does it matter now whether my cheek is rough or smooth? They say an unhappy man wants distractions—something to take him out of himself. Only as a dog-tired man wants an extra blanket on a cold night; he'd rather lie there shivering than get up and find one.

It's easy to see why the lonely become untidy, finally, dirty and disgusting.[22]

The tough, fibrous outer layer of the human heart—our preoccupation with earthly pursuits, pleasures, and ambitions—cracks and softens under the weight of grief. And once our earthly cares crack, we learn something about Joy. It was never an object on the move, looking for a way to get to us, like a knife in the hand of a pacing combatant or a hummingbird buzzing around our heads. It was a stab of light, not a stab from a blade. When the Joy pierced through the ordinary moments, it was a hole being punched in the roof. The light was always there, but the busyness of our daily lives had built a roof over our hearts and blocked it out.

But then, occasionally, something in our world, something beneath the roof—a poem, a book, a memory from childhood, a sunset on a spring day—would leap up and pop a little hole in the ceiling. A beam of light would then strike us, and it would feel like a knife blade cutting us with intense Longing, but it was simply the heat and brightness of something that had always been shining.

Our eyes often sting when we step out of a dark room.

Grief, therefore, exposes the nature of Joy. It is not a stab. It is more like a star. It is fixed high above, always shimmering—like the sparkling arpeggio of the guitar in the first minute of "Where The Streets Have No Name." It is a Deep Longing. I can't help but think of Lewis' Space Trilogy, how the characters speak of "Deep Heaven" when they gaze at the solar system and the stars and talk longingly of the spiritual realms beyond this world, unpolluted by evil.[23]

Suffering tends to remove the protective layers that we place between our hearts and Deep Longing, and this begs a question. If Joy's intense longing—"an unsatisfied desire which is itself more desirable than any other satisfaction"—were such a desirable experience, why would we intentionally, or even subconsciously, build a roof over our heads to block its light? Consider this startling observation from Lewis:

> I call it Joy, which is here a technical term and must be sharply distinguished both from Happiness and from Pleasure. Joy (in my sense) has indeed one characteristic, and one only, in common with them; the fact that anyone who has experienced it will want it again. Apart from that, and considered only in its quality, it might almost equally well be called a particular kind of unhappiness or grief. But then it is a kind we want. I doubt whether anyone who has tasted it would ever, if both were in his power, exchange it for all the pleasures in our world. But then Joy is never in our power and pleasure often is.[24]

In the ordinary seasons of life, we can never marshal Joy's power at will. We can never control it like we do Pleasure. It always has to catch us by surprise. We can reawaken it from time to time if the Longing came through something like a book or a movie that we could re-experience at will—though, even then, the second time is dimmer and muted because we're forcing it.

In a letter discovered and made public in 2014, C. S. Lewis writes about the difference between Joy and Pleasure to someone named Mrs. Ellis. The letter, dated August 19, 1945, was discovered in an old copy of *The Problem of Pain*. The letter pre-dates Lewis' *Surprised by Joy* autobiography. These are some of his earliest written thoughts on the subject: "Real joy seems to me almost as unlike security or prosperity as it is unlike agony. It jumps under one's ribs and tickles down one's back and makes one forget meals and keeps one (delightedly) sleepless o' nights. It shocks one awake where the other puts one to sleep. My private table is one second of Joy is worth twelve hours of Pleasure." And then in the postscript, he writes: "Don't you know the disappointment when you expected joy from a piece of music and get only pleasure? Like finding Leah when you thought you'd married Rachel!"[25]

After Joy leaves, when the heart searches for this Joy again but finds only Pleasure, restlessness comes. A disappointment settles over the mind. We then go searching for cheap substitutes that we can control. We get busy. We become fixated on lesser joys. Before long we've built a roof over our heads, and the light of that Longing seems dimmer now, if not totally blocked.

Unearthly Comforts

Blessed are those who mourn, for they shall be comforted.
– Matthew 5:4

In seasons of suffering, heaven does something special for us. God gives us a come-as-you-please access to Joy. Its powerful experience of Longing sits brightly in his hand—a ready tool forged to comfort us. In the ordinary seasons of life, these Stabs of Longing have to break through the noise, and only in fleeting moments.

But in grief, the Stabs behave more like starlight; they become fixed, ever present, shimmering high above and visible to us whenever we choose to look up. In times of trouble, the night is dark and cold, but at least we can see the stars. A Deep Longing, slow and grand, moves in, and its shimmering vigil above our heads and in the back of our minds has a purpose.

What that means in practical terms is that we should pay attention to the Longing as often as possible. When pangs of sorrow strike—whether we're remembering a loved one who has passed away or reliving the loss of something precious to us—that's when we look for the starlight hidden somewhere above the smoke. Somewhere in the sorrow it waits: that strange homesickness—the Deep Longing that pines for something that nothing in this world can satisfy.

We shouldn't distract ourselves with our worldly cares and rebuild the roof. We should chart our course by the bittersweet light of Longing and allow it to sting bright in our chests. We should let it stir us to action. If we do that, then we become pilgrims walking through the night, always looking up at the stars to find our bearings. Like the chords of U2's organ moving beneath the fixed brightness of the guitar, we move with faith beneath the constellations. We walk with confidence, knowing that this strange, otherworldly Longing in our hearts has a purpose.

Not Alone

When Bono finally enters and sings the lyrics for "Where The Streets Have No Name," he provides a hint of what will come next in our pilgrimage through the Stages of Joy. He paints a panoramic picture of someone searching through the plains of the high desert, looking for refuge from a poisonous storm, looking for a city that has no street signs—a nameless home.

Bono, whether he knows it or not, is describing the first Stage of Joy perfectly. All of the imagery and motion of the Deep Longing is there: movement toward something far off and unspecified, something shimmering on a lineless horizon. There's a larger narrative, a grand quest story unfolding—an epic marathon. Psalm 119:32 becomes appropriate here: "I will run the course of Your commandments, for You shall enlarge my heart." The Author who has the power to enlarge our hearts is writing an opus, not vignettes, and it's not all about us.

We will not be alone.

As Bono's words at the end of "Where The Streets Have No Name" suggest, our next stop on the journey is a rendezvous.

The solo quest will become a companion quest.

The Stages of Joy Playlist[26]

1. "Where The Streets Have No Name" from the album *The Joshua Tree*. Summary: in grief, Joy changes from temporary Stabs to a Deep Longing, expansive and abiding. This creates an inconsolable motion in our lives that takes us on a quest, if we allow it.

Scripture

"Blessed are those who mourn, for they shall be comforted" (Matt. 5:4).

Notes for the Quest

God comforts us in many ways. One of those ways comes through a deeper Longing that he makes available to us during times of sorrow. Grief softens our hearts and causes Joy to become readily available. The Deep Longing then bids us to keep moving forward on our quest.

If we're willing to take hold of that Deep Longing, if we're willing to look up, the solace that a pilgrim feels beneath the beauty of the stars at night will soothe us. The heavens remind pilgrims of a grandness that overshadows their journey, and the constellations provide a compass for sailors and travelers. In a similar way, Joy and its Deep Longing becomes a compass in the night.

A Prayer for the Journey

Abba Father, thank you for comforting me with Joy during my grief. Thank you for using seasons of sorrow to increase the Deep Longing. Deliver me from building a roof of worldly distractions that block out that Longing's starlight. Help me to keep my eyes fixed on your Joy, just as the pilgrim and the mariner keep their eyes fixed on the stars to maintain their sense of direction. In Jesus' name, amen.

More Bible Verses for the Road

Matthew 5:4; Psalm 119:32

CHAPTER 3

UNKNOWN CALLER:
THE HOUSE OF LONGING

*But you, when you pray, go into your room,
and when you have shut your door, pray to your
Father who is in the secret place; and your Father who
sees in secret will reward you openly.*
– Matthew 6:6

Song to cue: "Unknown Caller"
from the album *No Line On The Horizon*

The simple act of shutting a door has been a sufficient weapon for people to overthrow kingdoms, face the fire of martyrdom, and push back the fury of hell.

The act of shutting a door figures greatly in God's plan. When the Bible speaks of the secret place, it describes a private communion with God that happens when you go somewhere alone, when you shut the door behind you and spend raw, unscripted time with him. Jesus uses specific language to pinpoint when this begins: "when you have shut your door." The moment you close the door, a state of separation occurs between you and all else; the togetherness of your heart and your Father's begins.

But not all secret places are physical rooms.

Suffering and all its decorum—grief, anger, sadness, and loneliness—come together to build a secret place too. Suffering, whether we want it to or not, creates a veil of separation. It's a quarantine zone that separates us from society because no one— no other person, angel, or demon—has God's ability to look into our mind, know our thoughts, and experience firsthand our suffering twenty-four hours a day, seven days a week.

A Fireside Chat with God

Many in the secular West would be astonished to discover the beating heart of the Bible's claims: that God not only exists as a conscious, single-minded Personality, with the full scope of Individual Personhood applying, but that the Creator also longs for your personality to interact with his using the same tools that all other personalities use, such as conversation, the exchange of thought and emotion, and the bond of togetherness—sometimes even just the simple, quiet state of being in the same room together.

And then the Bible takes it a step further: not just the same room. No, the God of the Bible—the Father, the Son, and the Holy Spirit—wants to live, quite literally, inside you. Your thoughts and emotions become a fellowship hall, a room where, if you choose, you can shut the door behind you, meet with God to talk or perhaps just sit in silence, and enjoy the togetherness before a winter's hearth.

Grief brings winter, yes. And when you enter its manor, you

find yourself sitting in cold, empty rooms with unlit fireplaces. No matches or logs. But togetherness with Yahweh, the personal God of the Bible, brings fire to the hearth.

A Simple Response to a Simple Command

Your time in the secret place is not a bonus level or a self-improvement add-on to the seven habits of highly successful spirituality. It is the beating heart of a relationship, and God expects it. His instructions in Matthew 6:6 about going into the secret place to pray are commands, not suggestions.

However, though he commands it, he does not force it. Your free will must permit his entry before he can begin his work. But if you believe Jesus' claims that he is God; if you believe in what he did on the cross and in the tomb for you; if you have the childlike audacity to speak to him directly and invite him to take up residence in your experience of suffering—even with the simplest prayer, "Jesus, I invite you into my experience of suffering; enter into the darkest corners of my heart and allow me to encounter you in this lonely place"—then the Great Carpenter will come. However, he will not come to wave a magic wand and dissolve your problems into the ether. He will come with his carpenter tools—to work.

He will come to labor day and night and remodel your quarantined, private house of suffering into something new. He will change it into a sacred meeting place. As Jesus said, "Anyone who loves me will obey my teaching. My Father will love them, and we will come to them and make our home with them" (John 14:23 NIV).

Once you stumble upon this treasure hidden in the night,

when you see how the great sufferings of life become a secret room of communion, everything flips upside down. Night becomes day. Moments of indescribable sorrow also contain bright stars of Joy. And they have purpose. You're moving along an important path toward something. He began with the fleeting Stabs of Joy, and then he moved to the expansive Deep Longing, remote and abiding like a star.

But now, through the time you spend in secret togetherness with him, he is building a House hidden in the night.

It is a permanent structure of longing that encloses us in close quarters, more intimate than the wide panorama of Deep Longing and more enduring than the Stabs. The House of Longing, as he continues to build it, will be as expansive as the shadowy manor of grief that rises over us. In fact, the House of Longing will be bigger.

But to inhabit such a place, we must press on and yield to the inconsolable motion—the continual aches of Longing that pepper the day and glow blue in the night—and we must surrender our time, stop our busy work, and go to God in the secret place whenever the Longing moves us, even when we have nothing to bring him but our wounds. My late mother Sally described it this way, in a prayer written to God:

> Our words are leafy, windblown attempts to attach meaning to your Tree of Life. You are the nourishing source for our frailty, yet we disengage from your security and flitter away into gusts and puddles, mud banks and debris. Odd, how we seek beauty and food in transient things. When I flutter to the ground, exhausted, bent, and bruised, you

gather me up in a whispering breeze, and you rest my droopy form upon your limbs. Comforted and nourished, I peek at the world of busyness and rest.[1]

Avoiding the Secret Place Like the Plague: The Siren Song of the West

Getting to that secret safe haven in God is not always easy. We must not forget that the Great Carpenter builds the House of Longing within the House of Grief. If we avoid the grieving process at all costs, we avoid the secret place too. The West spends millions of dollars every year doing all it can to avoid such things. Our raw craving for distraction, for anything that will make us forget about our suffering and mortality, has found its paradise in this new millennium's screen age. We dread the house of sorrow and grief, and our pop culture works overtime to keep it at a safe distance. It's frightening how well it succeeds. But no matter how many people or screens we gather around us, a corner of the heart still stings with frostbite and vacancy. This emptiness—the darkened room, that dreaded lair of shadows where we must go alone, where no soul can enter with us—terrifies the Western mind.

But this is the very place where we must begin if God is to bring an end to our winter.

Text Messages from God: When the Unknown Caller Beckons

When U2 recorded the song "Unknown Caller" in the city of Fez, Morocco, for their twelfth studio album, *No Line On The Horizon*, all four members of the band gathered under the open sky of a riad, a traditional Moroccan home that has an open-roofed courtyard or garden in the middle.[2] And when I heard the band play the song at the Rose Bowl in October 2009, Bono said this about that recording experience: "It was a beautiful sunrise on that morning....Two birds flew into our little riad, and we wrote this song. It's called 'Unknown Caller.' For a chorus of voices. A chorus of voices! Help me!"

According to a sixty-four-page interview with U2, which was published as a magazine and released with *No Line On The Horizon*,[3] "Unknown Caller" tells the story of a broken man who receives mysterious text messages on his phone even though he has no signal; and the song strongly implies that God has sent the messages.

With fantastical images that would fit right in with the clocks melting in Salvador Dali's Surrealist painting, Bono weaves a sense of mystery, even eeriness, as a person receives text messages from God in the middle of the night. As the song's chorus shouts, God extends a simple invitation to the broken man. It could be summarized this way: Come to me, and I will make all things new. Draw near to me and begin a journey beyond your obsessive orbit of Self.

Music journalists have noted that "Unknown Caller" references Jeremiah 33:3,[4] which says, "Call to me and I will answer you and tell you great and unsearchable things you do not know" (NIV). In 2001, Bono explained to *Rolling Stone* that he refers to that verse as "God's phone number," which was why he had the album cover for *All That You Can't Leave Behind* edited to include "J333."[5]

"Unknown Caller" certainly feels like an invitation. It haunts you. It beckons, pleads, and pulls. It yearns for something beyond this world—what C. S. Lewis called the "severe" and "remote" when describing the sublime longing of Joy.[6]

What's astonishing, however, is how the music communicates these themes as clearly as the lyrics—perhaps even more so.

A Metaphor for Valleys and Mountains

After the 2009 Rose Bowl concert, when Bono mentioned how two birds flew into their riad, I went home, listened to "Unknown Caller," and turned up the volume so I could hear the birds. Sure enough, a joyful chirping fills the early seconds of the song. The Edge plays a few opening notes on his guitar—a sparse, warm G-major chord—and joins the birds. That same morning they recorded, a beautiful sunrise greeted them in their open-roofed courtyard—another thing that Bono had mentioned at the concert. The song's introduction imitates this creeping warmth of dawn and the flutter of life coming awake.

As the music stirs itself into morning, The Edge does something simple but effective with his guitar work: he emphasizes two notes, the G and the D, and they create the same 3:2 frequency ratio we hear in "Where The Streets Have No Name," a harmony that delights the human brain with perfect consonance. Music theorists call this ratio a "perfect fifth" because it creates a sense of enormous stability, like the colossal pillars of a temple. For this reason, it is one of the most beloved chords in music history. (In fact, this ratio is one of the first things we hear in the opening notes of the famous *Star Wars* theme, one of the most colossal music pieces ever written.)

It's not that U2 is doing something uncommon by using

this perfect chord. It's how they use it in their song structures and production that makes a difference. In the opening of "Unknown Caller," The Edge barely alights on this perfect harmony, without stirring any of its colossal power. After a few seconds, it builds until, at 0:57, the drummer comes in with toms that beat a steady momentum.

Then, at 1:16, with a crash of a cymbal, the full band explodes with sound. Amplifiers awake with distortion as the drummer splashes and strikes along with the bass. They're not just playing anything, however; they're restating the guitar's quiet theme and expanding it. They're shouting what the guitar had been whispering only a moment before.

And then, almost as quickly as the explosion happens, the power dies, and the band quiets into a hushed, anxious verse. Bono enters and sings about the man who gets a mysterious phone call from an unknown caller in the middle of the night; text messages appear on his phone's screen even though there's no signal.

God is sending a message.

As Bono explores this appearance of the Unknown Caller in the lyrical themes, the music tells its own story. It does something very different from the glorious sunrise that started the song. It descends, sinking down into darkness. It returns to the mist and blue shadows of night.

In fact, the bass guitar and synths are, quite literally, descending into what music textbooks would call "stepwise motion," as if the notes were walking carefully down a staircase step-by-step. (The first theorists of Western music used the metaphorical term "steps" to describe the way notes can move up or down in small increments of motion. In fact, musicians invented the piano to organize these "steps" into a neatly ordered visual space: white and black keys placed in a clean line.)

The two instruments step down into the dark as Bono sings about clocks melting and text messages appearing without a signal. In the middle of all this motion and mystery, The Edge plays a static pattern of notes, slightly distorted and pensive, above the descending instruments. His unwavering high notes allow the sinking motion of the other instruments to stand out. It makes us feel the sinking in our gut, and it feels strange at first. After such a glorious sunrise in the introduction, the song sinks to its knees in the dark.

In the second verse, the descending motion comes again, but heavier. A new guitar part traces the downward line with doomsday distortion as if it were descending into the Abyss.

Then, in a moment of epiphany, just as the descending instruments hit their lowest note, the whole band jumps back to the shining G-major chord used in the opening sunrise. But this time everything is bigger. A chorus of voices shout-sing a high D above the G, a colossal perfect fifth—the same perfect fifth hinted at in the guitar's wispy introduction. Now they are shouting it from the rooftops. The hugeness of the sound towers over the stereo field. It's not the light of dawn anymore; it's a noonday sun at full strength breaking through a cloud when you least expect it.

The sink-then-leap architecture of "Unknown Caller" tells a story that helps us understand the Stages of Joy. As we go about daily life, God pushes our hearts out of stagnation with Deep Longing. These aches move us from our distracted thoughts and busy work and send us into the secret place of prayer, literally or figuratively. That moment of departure into the secret place can be like the hint of sunrise we hear in the beginning of "Unknown Caller"—the birds chirping merrily in the weak, new light. A new cheerfulness sprinkles our hearts as we leave our labors and walk toward the secret place to pray.

But when the prayer begins, when we sink to our knees, shadows swallow us up like a dark valley. We're descending, not rising. The prayer becomes work, and it doesn't seem to be doing anything. It might even be painful, as the solitude brings the sting of wounds to mind.

Even so, as we cast our cares at his feet, as we press on with persistence in the secret place and walk patiently through the valley, neither giving up nor turning back—always remembering the Bible's promise, "Draw near to God and He will draw near to you" (James 4:8)—then, sooner or later, stairs appear and take us to the mountain peak. Just as the music in "Unknown Caller" leaps from the valley to the mountain of the perfect fifth, God lifts our hearts onto his shoulders.

And our new elevation changes everything.

A Lion's Face Hiding in the Shadows: What We Find at the New Elevation

When we reach this new elevation, the most important thing we discover is not something new about ourselves, but about God. This something new might surprise us as it once surprised a boy named Digory. In Lewis' *The Magician's Nephew*, Digory is full of sorrow because his mother is dying of an illness. One day he stumbles into Narnia and causes a disaster. When Digory stands before Aslan to give account for what he has done, Aslan commands him to perform a quest.

Digory, whose only desire is to find some magic that will cure his mother's terminal illness, tells Aslan about his mother. The boy even considers trying to strike a bargain with the Lion, but he realizes that "the Lion was not at all the sort of person one could try to make bargains with."[7] When Digory, who is certain that the Lion will ignore the plea about his mother, looks Aslan in the face for the first time, he discovers something shocking:

> Up till then he had been looking at the Lion's great feet and the huge claws on them; now, in his despair, he looked up at its face. What he saw surprised him as much as anything in his whole life. For the tawny face was bent down near his own and (wonder of wonders) great shining tears stood in the Lion's eyes. They were such big, bright tears compared with Digory's own that for a moment he felt as if the Lion must really be sorrier about his Mother than he was himself.[8]

After Digory sees this miracle in the eyes of the Lion, he agrees to the quest. Aslan then does something remarkable: "The Lion drew a deep breath, stooped its head even lower and gave him a Lion's kiss. And at once Digory felt that new strength and courage had gone into him."[9]

In the House of Longing, we meet Aslan as Digory did. When we see his face, new strength fills us, and we have a revelation: Our painful circumstances hurt him more than they hurt us. He grieves for our loved ones and our sad circumstances more than we do.

How can this be? How can God feel our pain as if it were his own, as if he were suffering more than us?

Because he is suffering more than us.

Our broken spiritual condition numbs the heart in more ways than we can imagine. Even the most emotionally sensitive person functions at a lower level when compared to God's perfectly keen emotional state. We each find ways to cope with our circumstances, to dull the pain and make it bearable. But God never dulls his senses or pushes our pain away. When they tried to give Jesus something to numb the pain of the cross (Matt. 27:34), he refused. He perceives our pain with perfect clarity and dives headfirst into the black depths, even if they plunge as deep as the Mariana Trench.

But this life-changing truth about God's love must not stay an abstraction in our heads—a picture in our imagination. It must move from our minds to a full-bodied revelation in our hearts. This begins to happen when we make the House of Longing our home.

And that's not always an easy task.

The House of Longing is Not a Formula

During a difficult season, I once became so frustrated with the constant exhaustion of emotional pain and so desperate for relief that I locked myself in a bathroom and prayed a rather outrageous prayer to God: "I will not leave here until you come and meet with me."

To be honest, I'm not sure how long I would have stuck

it out. But God was merciful. Although he tested my resolve, eventually he arrived. Like that perfect-fifth chord that breaks the darkness in "Unknown Caller," the heaviness in my heart suddenly lifted. My vision cleared. His Presence—an actual physical presence that in some inexplicable way felt near in proximity to my senses—filled that bathroom with such heaviness that I dared not stand.

My knees felt too weak. The air around me, the very fabric of space and time, felt as if it were bending under his weight. I wondered if the walls would crack. It reminded me of the final scene in Lewis' *That Hideous Strength* when a presence from Deep Heaven descended and "lay upon the house, or even on the whole Earth, with a cold pressure such as might flatten the very orb of Tellus to a wafer."[10]

Of course, such a glorious encounter that has something "physical," if that is even an applicable word, is not my point. Neither is it a necessity. The majority of my most life-changing breakthroughs in my relationship with God have come in the midst of the most ordinary, non-glorious circumstances. His nearness and his work in my heart was the important thing—more important than any physical sensation. In that moment in the secret place, he was clearing away the debris in my relationship with him.

Why would he have to do that?

It's simple, really. My selfish nature, which tends to bend in on itself unless an external force intervenes, does not mix well with suffering. The two blend like mud and snow until a disgusting gray slush covers everything. The iciness of sorrow, when mixed with self-centeredness, numbs our heart-to-heart relationship with God and freezes our understanding of his truths.

As I waited there for him in that small room, he changed his Word from distant intellectual propositions to hot-blooded revelations that electrified my intellect and emotions. We were communing. It was a conversation. The relationship had come back to life.

I should also clarify one other point: there is no formula. This is not a works-based system in which God stands by waiting until you've put in a requisite amount of time on the clock before he shows up. There have been times when God arrived the moment I stepped into the secret place, before I even had a chance to say hello. There have been other times when weeks have passed before any discernible breakthrough came. There have been times when I wasn't seeking him at all, and he showed up and knocked me over with a revelation from his Word just because he felt like it.

I am not prescribing a formula for personal achievement; I am presenting a principle for healthy relationship. Draw near to him with persistent, real hunger, and he will draw near to you. When and how he draws near to you are his prerogative. Your job is to seek and wait, and then seek and wait some more.

The time spent in the secret place uncovers the next clue: the House of Longing has a peculiar feature. A passage from the book *The Last Battle* describes this feature well. When the Narnian character Tirian steps into a stable, which is really a portal to a different world, something amazing happens:

He looked round again and could hardly believe his eyes. There was the blue sky overhead, and grassy country spreading as far as he could see in every direction, and his new friends all round him laughing. "It seems, then," said Tirian, smiling himself, "that the stable seen from within and the stable seen from without are two different places."

"Yes," said the Lord Digory. "Its inside is bigger than its outside."[11]

Not only do we find Someone waiting for us in the secret place, but we also find a Door. This Door opens to a new kingdom that has no anchor in this world. As we sink to our knees in prayer, thinking that the secret place is a small, cramped room, instead we find a great country sprawling before us.

The inside is bigger than the outside.

The Stages of Joy Playlist

2. "Unknown Caller" from the album *No Line On The Horizon*. Summary: the quest begins with a rendezvous with God in the secret place. He uses Deep Longing to draw us into a place of abiding communion with him—the House of Longing.

Scripture

"Draw near to God and He will draw near to you" (James 4:8).

Notes for the Quest

The world is full of closed doors, VIP-only access areas, and lofty skyscrapers filled with executive offices—places where only the most successful people are allowed to breathe the rarified air. This world's closed-door policy can make us so accustomed to restricted access that when a door swings open before us, we do not know what to do with it.

The open door in James 4:8 is by far the biggest one in history. It is too precious to ignore. Yet so many millions, both religious and non-religious, have ignored the door that Christ tore open on the cross. Many people have gone their entire lives without ever knowing what it's like to hungrily draw near to God until He draws near to them.

We've been handed the most precious invitation in the world. What we do with that invitation will alter the course of our lives. It is an open door that we should not walk away from.

A Prayer for the Journey

Abba Father, save me from shallow contentedness and lazy complacency. Increase my hunger for you, and let that hunger triumph over inaction. Help my unbelief, and guard me from the cynicism of this broken world that doesn't dare believe in the grandness of your promises. Fill me with a sure confidence and childlike faith in the door that you've opened to anyone bold enough to run through. In Jesus' name, amen.

More Bible Verses for the Road

Matthew 6:6; John 14:23; Matthew 27:34

PART II

CITY OF BLINDING LIGHTS
AND OPEN WINDOWS
TO HEAVEN

WHERE WE ARE ON THE MAP:
A SUMMARY OF PART I

- C. S. Lewis described a different kind of Joy than what the world knows. It is neither Happiness nor Pleasure, and it has more in common with grief; it produces an intense longing for something unnamed and far off. The sensation of Joy's otherworldly longing is more desirable than any fleeting pleasure that can be had in this world.

- In grief, this special Joy changes from temporary Stabs to a Deep Longing, expansive and abiding. This creates an inconsolable motion in our lives that takes us on a quest.

- The quest begins with a rendezvous with God in the secret place. He uses Deep Longing to draw us into a place of communion with him—the House of Longing, which is a secret place where we meet with God, a place unseen and overlooked by the world. This House also has a Door, which opens to the next stage of our journey.

CHAPTER 4

BLINDING LIGHTS AND UNBENDING GRASS: A TRIP TO HEAVEN

Song to cue: "City Of Blinding Lights"
from the album *How To Dismantle An Atomic Bomb*

The barrier between heaven and earth felt paper-thin on the day of my mother's funeral. She was buried in a cemetery in Southern California, and when we drove home after the service, a rare sight greeted us: clear skies over Los Angeles—not a speck of smog anywhere.

On the brim of the valley, mountains stood over the freeway to inspect cars and showcase triumphant white spires. These same snowy peaks had lined themselves up on the horizon like soldiers and presided over the cemetery during the funeral. As we sang a worship song next to my mom's pink casket, gusts of ice-chilled air swept through the trees and touched our faces in the sun. The mountains had given their breezes to us gift-wrapped and tied with a bow, a proper salute for a woman who had spent much of her life backpacking.

All of it—the mountains, the snow-capped peaks and breezes—filled me with a Deep Longing that lasted into the night and brooded beneath the moonlight. It moved me into the secret House of Longing to seek God's face, a place unseen and overlooked by the world. As this happened, the fabric of our world's reality—the fading space-time blanket that enwraps us—grew as thin as a sheet of wax paper.

The physical world felt less like ultimate reality. I had the strange sensation of living inside a cardboard box that had been painted to look like a castle—the kind a child would build with great relish—while, all the time, my little cardboard box was sitting inside the great hall of a real castle. There was a distinct sense of something larger and permanent peeking through chinks in the physical world.

Around that time, I came across a passage from Lewis' *The Last Battle*, and my spirit leaped with recognition; Lewis had put in words what I was sensing intuitively. In the passage, the Pevensies—Lucy, Edmund, and Peter—enter Aslan's Country. They discover something that is, at first, devastating. The Narnia they had known when they were young had been destroyed. But then they find something remarkable: the Narnia that was lost is there in Aslan's Country—only, it is the true Narnia.

When Peter marvels how it's possible to be in Narnia again—and to feel that it is the real Narnia—Digory, who has joined their company, gives this stunning reply:

When Aslan said you could never go back to Narnia, he meant the Narnia you were thinking of. But that was not the real Narnia. That had a beginning and an end.

It was only a shadow or a copy of the real Narnia which has always been here and always will be here: just as our own world, England and all, is only a shadow or copy of something in Aslan's real world. You need not mourn over Narnia, Lucy. All of the old Narnia that mattered, all the dear creatures, have been drawn into the real Narnia through the Door. And of course it is different; as different as a real thing is from a shadow or as waking life is from a dream.[1]

When heaven invades our little cardboard palace, the busy activities and earthly plans that have so madly absorbed our attention lose their weightiness. Their appearance as ultimate reality—as convincing and plausible as it seems—is exposed as a shoddy paint job over a cardboard facade.

But something much larger and more solid is moving in—or coming down, more accurately. We are "pulling down deep Heaven on [our] heads,"[2] as Lewis writes in *That Hideous Strength*—though, unlike the villains in the novel, we are pulling it down to our Joy, not our despair.

Heaven On Earth

Sometimes we forget that the book of Revelation—that great prophetic book that has loomed over the chasm of history these past two thousand years and still towers over the modern mind—describes heaven coming down to earth. Earth does not go up to heaven in the end. The Western mind has developed a troubling idea of heaven: disembodied souls hovering in a vague ether of light—a bright but bland and bodiless glow.

Western Christians, in other words, imagine heaven obliterating all matter. But God will heal and restore what he has made; in fact, heaven will come down to earth and remake it. Timothy Keller, in his sermon "The New Heaven and New Earth," which he preached at Redeemer Presbyterian Church in April 2009, said this about the book of Revelation's vision of heaven:

> Those two words [coming down] changed my life years ago…because here's John the Apostle getting a vision of the future—of the end of time, of the end of history—and what does he see at the end of history? It's not individual souls rising up and escaping this material world…what you have is Heaven coming down and transforming the earth. That's the reason we can say that the resurrected Christ is the First Fruits.[3]

Keller then notes that when Jesus rose from the dead, he had a physical body designed to function in an earthly environment. He ate fish. He let people touch and embrace him. Jesus was not a ghost, in other words. And if Jesus is the first fruits of what's to come, we will have perfected bodies too. God has no intentions of getting rid of the material universe. He's coming to heal it, as we see in Revelation 21:1–4: "Now I saw a new heaven and a new earth, for the first heaven and the first earth had passed away….And I heard a loud voice from heaven saying, 'Behold, the tabernacle of God is with men, and He will dwell with them, and they shall be His people….And God will wipe away every tear from their eyes; there shall be no more death, nor sorrow, nor crying. There shall be no more pain, for the former things have passed away.'"

Perhaps one of the greatest portraits of this truth in literature is C. S. Lewis' *The Great Divorce*. This short novel conducts a thought experiment: what would happen if souls from hell were permitted to take a bus trip to the outskirts of heaven's country and taste a sample of its glory for a day? As we go along for the ride, Lewis shows the reader a heaven that has such solidity in contrast to hell that when a spirit from hell tries to visit heaven, it can't walk on the grass. The grass blades are like swords beneath the spirit's feet, and the grass won't bend under the spirit's weight; it doesn't have enough solidity in heaven. It's as if all other domains outside of heaven—whether hell or the fallen earth—are shadows cast beneath heaven's permanent, behemoth mass.

The narrator in *The Great Divorce*, one of the spirits who is visiting heaven, describes his experience: "The grass, hard as diamonds to my unsubstantial feet, made me feel as if I were walking on wrinkled rock, and I suffered pains like those of the mermaid in Hans Andersen. A bird ran across in front of me and I envied it. It belonged to that country and was as real as the grass."[4]

The Great Divorce takes place just before the "sunrise that shoots Time dead"[5]—presumably the dawn of eternity when history ends. However, we don't have to wait until that great dawn to get glimpses of the truth. The unshakable reality of heaven is not cordoned off to a holding cell at the end of time. It breaks into the now. In our present lives we see hints of heaven and the startling nearness of eternity in the humdrum moments. We sense that Jesus really meant it when he told us to pray, "Your kingdom come, your will be done, on earth as it is in heaven" (Matt. 6:10 NIV).

After my mother's funeral, it took some time to adjust to this experiential understanding of heaven—that it breaks into our reality with urgency. Heaven seems eager to carve shavings of its glory on our heads. It invades our world, and the fleeting Stabs of Longing and the abiding Deep Longing are signs of this. This invasion, this new awareness of heaven's reality, has a specific purpose: to keep us alert to a tension that hovers over our days.

Interestingly, we stumble upon a picture of this tension in a song about the people of New York City.

A Sea of Faces:
The Blinding Beauty of U2's "City Of Blinding Lights"

The lyrical idea for the chorus of U2's "City Of Blinding Lights" came to Bono shortly after 9/11. It happened during a concert in New York City, when the city was still in shock about the tragedy that had just happened. As the lights shined on the faces of the audience, he saw people simultaneously weeping and triumphantly singing and shouting along to "Where The Streets Have No Name."

At that moment, he realized how much the concert was helping the people work through their grief. He saw in their faces a resolve to work through the pain. The chorus of "City Of Blinding Lights" describes how beautiful that moment was for him as he looked out and saw a sea of faces overwhelmed with both sorrow and hope.[6]

Musically, "City Of Blinding Lights" has one of the band's

most well-known and beloved approaches to a musical introduction: a gradual building of sound, followed by an explosion
of inconsolable motion as we hear in "Where The Streets Have
No Name." After this explosion of life, we hear yet another
classic U2 trademark: a sonorous piano playing a lonely, contemplative melodic line over a driving beat. The piano's notes,
mixed with a swooning slide guitar, find a jet stream above the
band's steady rhythm below.

U2 first captured this yearning sound with "New Year's Day"
in 1983. Their 2004 album, called *How To Dismantle An Atomic
Bomb*, was, in some ways, a return to those early eighties roots,
and "City Of Blinding Lights" encouraged that association. As
in "New Year's Day," its bittersweet longing in the piano builds
toward the chorus. But this is where "City of Blinding Lights"
finds its own path. Once the chorus arrives, it leaves the brooding mellowness and explodes with a shout-sing exultation.

At this point, Bono sings a six-word melody that carves a
distinct, soaring shape in the air. For the first four notes, the
musicians move against each other. Adam, on the bass, moves
in contrary motion to Bono's melody. Adam starts low and
walks up the stairs, while Bono's tenor starts high and walks
down the stairs. The two meet in the middle where The Edge
has been hammering the notes of the same chord. And then
Bono hits the climactic note of his melody—the highest note—
and The Edge starts moving around too. The three musicians
nimbly shift around each other. It's a pulsating blast of melodies
carefully stepping around each other in a nuanced dance.

But in the big scheme of things—from the perspective of the
song's key—the chorus, despite all the movement, stays in one

spot, hovering around the perfect fifth (the V chord) and the perfect fourth (the IV chord) of the key. Anytime a song lingers around that general middle region of a key, it creates a special kind of tension in the ear. The listener desperately wants to hear it resolve to the root chord (also called the "tonic" or the "one chord," designated by the Roman numeral "I").

The root chord of the key provides the harmonic foundation for all of the other chords. In fact, the ear expects the music to resolve to the root chord at some point. By not doing so—by hovering around the middle area and delaying its return to home base—U2 creates tension. It promises a certain action, and then just as it's about to complete the action, it freezes.

It's similar to when two people are in love, and the girl leans in to kiss the guy but stops just before the kiss can happen. As the guy waits for her to resolve her suspension of movement, the tension grows unbearable. It's a similar sensation when a band delays the resolution of a chord progression that wants to go back to its root. It's a powerful tool, and it's effective. Your ear is begging for the melody and harmony to stop dancing around the middle and just land on the root notes.

The band does exactly that at 2:19. As Bono finishes his lyrical phrase, the band switches chords and resolves to the root of the key. And then every element—Bono's exultant melody, Adam's relentless bass notes, and The Edge's sprinting guitar chords—exhales into a long sigh. A tremendous release relaxes every tendon in the song. Notes of longing ring above the band again, and Bono returns and quietly sings the song's title—a contemplative punctuation to the Stab of Joy that had just engulfed him.

Suspended in Tension

"City Of Blinding Lights" becomes a parable: life in this fallen world hovers in the tension of a suspended chord progression, and it longs with a sickeningly intense desire for the chords to resolve. The only resolution big enough to resolve that tension is the new heaven and the new earth. Possibly the greatest lie that anyone can believe is that this finite, fragile, short-circuited life in our world could ever fully resolve the tension from its own resources. Yet we build our identity around the things of this world: career, family, health, politics, security, and wealth. The many pursuits under the sun swallow our vision whole, and those things become all we see; they become a city of blinding lights.

They become reality.

But the unceasing discontent in our souls—a restless longing that never leaves, even when we get everything we want in life—points to a greater reality. As Lewis writes in *Mere Christianity*, "If I find in myself a desire which no experience in this world can satisfy, the most probable explanation is that I was made for another world. If none of my earthly pleasures satisfy it, that does not prove that the universe is a fraud. Probably earthly pleasures were never meant to satisfy it, but only to arouse it, to suggest the real thing."[7]

This world can trick us into thinking that there is no tension in our hearts that cannot be resolved with some earthly comfort or success. The danger comes when we lose sight of heaven—the chord ahead that is about to sound. The intrusions of Joy—the Stabs and the Deep Longing—and the sudden invasion of heaven's reality are there to remind us of the tension, the vast chord progression that still hovers over our days, waiting to be resolved.

It's there to make us feel our need for something more than what we see. We chase every gust of wind in this world, and we think it will fill the emptiness. As the Word says, "Yet when I surveyed all that my hands had done and what I had toiled to achieve, everything was meaningless, a chasing after the wind" (Eccl. 2:11 NIV). A howling wind might fill up a cave and make some noise for a moment, but the emptiness never goes away, and the wind just makes the cave walls colder.

Once we stop chasing the wind—once we allow the tension of heaven to fix our eyes on eternity—the next step in the journey uncovers something glorious. The House of Longing that God is building inside the sorrow, and the invasion of heaven that occurs there, is just the first step. Once heaven arrives, it gets to work on building an addition to the House.

To learn about this new addition, however, we must return to Narnia—this time to a place full of sunshine and water, where we can dunk our faces in a draught of liquid light.

The Stages of Joy Playlist

3. "City Of Blinding Lights" from the album *How To Dismantle An Atomic Bomb*. Summary: as we spend time in the House of Longing, heaven invades, and we fix our attention on the true reality that lies beyond the blinding lights of this world.

Scripture

"These all died in faith, not having received the promises, but having seen them afar off were assured of them, embraced them and confessed that they were strangers and pilgrims on the earth. For those who say such things declare plainly that they seek a homeland. And truly if they had called to mind that country from which they had come out, they would have had opportunity to return. But now they desire a better, that is, a heavenly country. Therefore God is not ashamed to be called their God, for He has prepared a city for them" (Heb. 11:13–16).

Notes for the Quest

Anyone who has had to leave home and family knows how sharp the blade of homesickness can be. Yet everything on this earth is temporary, even our beloved homes and families. The Scriptures call us to something startling: we are to have the same kind of sharp homesickness for heaven. The flurries of emotions and thoughts that fill our souls each day must be reorganized around this new homesickness. Yet it is not a far-off home. Our true home begins to invade even now, and it transforms how we live on this earth.

A Prayer for the Journey

Abba Father, take my old homesickness—the part of me that obsesses every day on all the interim pursuits, the happiness and pleasures of this world—and replace it with a new homesickness. Let heaven invade every corner of my life. Give me the eyes and the heart of the sojourning "strangers and pilgrims" who have fixed their eyes on the heavenly country. In Jesus' name, amen.

More Bible Verses for the Road

Revelation 21:1–4; Matthew 6:10; Ecclesiastes 2:11

CHAPTER 5

LIQUID LIGHT AND
A WINDOW IN THE SKIES

Song to cue: "Window In The Skies"
from the album *U218 Singles*

It was unexpected.

Many years ago, a Stab of Longing—that enormous swell of desire for something far off—came to me while I was drinking water.

But it wasn't just any water. It was mountain spring water piped into a cabin from a pristine high-country lake a few miles away. I was a child when, while standing in a humble two-room cabin in the wilderness, I held a glass with both hands and brought the icy perfection closer, trying not to spill a drop.

The moment just before I tasted the water, a burst of wind moved through the trees and in the open window, bringing a sharp, stinging smell of pine needles. As I drank, it felt as if everything around me—the pine forests, the blue sky, the millions of sparkles on the lakes—had taken liquid form, and all of that cool, brilliant perfection came together in my mouth.

My family was staying at a cabin in Virginia Lakes, a fishing resort and a popular trailhead in California's Sierra Nevada range. The many-colored lakes in that wilderness, with their distinct hues of blue, red, and emerald, curve through the winding mountains like a jeweled staircase. When you see the lakes from the top of the summit at fourteen thousand feet, they spread below you with a quiet showmanship. They look like gemstones set into the steep sides of mountains and forests, all rejoicing in the sun. In that moment, as you survey the wonder, it feels as if the light is transforming into liquid and the liquid is transforming into light, and you can drink it all in with the five senses.

The joy of drinking that water and seeing the lakes from the summit will be, most likely, the closest I come to enjoying what the sailors experienced in *The Voyage of the Dawn Treader*, the third book published in the Narnia Series. There is a moment in the adventure when, as they enter the waters close to Aslan's Country, King Caspian and his shipmates discover that the ocean is no longer salty. It has turned into something astounding:

The King took the bucket in both hands, raised it to his lips, sipped, then drank deeply and raised his head. His face was changed. Not only his eyes but everything about him seemed to be brighter.

"Yes," he said, "it is sweet. That's real water, that. I'm not sure that it isn't going to kill me. But it is the death I would have chosen—if I'd known about it till now."

"What do you mean?" asked Edmund.

"It—it's like light more than anything else," said Caspian.

"That is what it is," said Reepicheep. "Drinkable light. We must be very near the end of the world now."[1]

The idea of this drinkable light stirs something deep in the heart. Even though it's fiction, it grabs the heartstrings because it feels like a promise or a reflection of something that is true. Even in our ordinary experiences with water, there comes times when it's hard to tell if we're drinking water or sunshine. It's astonishing how water immerses the five senses in its splendor: we hear it murmuring in the stream or roaring on the beach; we taste its coolness; we feel it swirling around our skin; we smell it teeming with life—moss, stones, seaweed, driftwood; and we see it electrified with sparks and currents when the dawn hits it.

How can something so small and simple as a water molecule produce so much sensory abundance?

There is a simple explanation.

Accumulation. Water demonstrates the power of accumulation better than any other element.

In fact, even a modest accumulation of water can become so magnificent that it creates the illusion of infinitude. Its mirage of permanence only grows stronger the more you stare at it, as if you were staring into something beyond this world: "He has also set eternity in the human heart" (NIV), as Ecclesiastes 3:11 says. The sight of an ocean stretching hundreds of miles in either direction can stir unbearable pangs in the spirit. It awakens some secret eternity that God hid inside of us when he made us. We yearn for what large bodies of water only suggest: life-giving permanence—the feeling of rest and that relieved sigh that comes when we finally obtain something so glorious and vast in its presence that we're certain it could never be taken from us.

Even if we're non-religious and we don't long for heaven by name, we find something far off—our children and their futures, the conservation of natural wonders in the environment, or perhaps some cause or organization that's greater than ourselves that will go on after we die—and we extract whatever sense of blissful permanence from it that we can. Or we try to accumulate as much of something as possible: money, success in our careers, romance, true love, years of happy marriage, friends, badges of honor in the community, moral excellence, pleasurable hobbies, retirement funds—the list of earthly pursuits goes on. We strive to accumulate all these things because, like the sight of the ocean that seems to go on forever, their abundance creates an illusion of permanence.

This illusion makes the need for accumulation addictive. We strive our whole lives for that one special thing until, if we're fortunate, that thing, whatever it is, has been given to us in abundance. And then it surrounds us on every side and creates a feeling of happy permanence, even if it is only a feeling. The longing for that feeling to wash over us day and night becomes a quiet obsession.

It becomes the anchor of our identity.

But nothing in this world offers permanent rest. Money runs out (or we work ourselves to death trying to keep up with our need for it), promotions and careers come to an end, natural environments can be destroyed in the blink of an eye, children and grandchildren grow up and stop needing us, a single mistake stains our conscience and ruins our reputation of do-gooding, and all the pleasure in the arms of the beloved can't stop a one-night stand from turning into the morning after. Even the happiest marriage isn't enough to chase away the emptiness.

Nothing in this world satisfies. No earthly dream is permanent.

This is one reason why Lewis' idea of drinkable light can stir such a Deep Longing in our hearts. When King Caspian drinks it, the liquid light turns back mortal decay and revitalizes him with supernatural power. When we drink shimmering water as cool as the Arctic on a hot day, it's hard not to feel the same way, as if the water were healing our mortality and turning back time. We would give anything for that to be true. Although it's a work of imagination, Lewis' idea of supernatural liquid light has that ring of truth—a suggestion of something wonderful that never ends and that renews, sustains, and preserves our lives forever.

Jesus hinted at this reality when he spoke of fountains of living water springing up within the person who drank the water he had to give (John 4:13–14). When we understand and believe the claims he made about himself, and if we invite him to live inside of us, his living water will begin to flow. He promises it.

And he brings a new kind of accumulation.

When our awareness of this new accumulation grows, when we learn to drink from it daily, we will stop gnawing at the grubby roots of this world. Instead of contenting ourselves with mud pies, we will look skyward; we will drink from the rootlets that dangle from heaven.

Fortunately, there is a practical meaning behind all the imagery. Strangely enough—and I never would have expected to veer in this direction—our modern era's computer age provides the perfect analogy to unlock the practical meaning.

Heaven's Auto-Save Function: The Infinite Cloud Drive

Most computer applications that involve any kind of important work have an auto-save feature; as you're working, the computer automatically saves a copy of your document. If the program crashes, you won't lose anything if you forgot to save it. It's an old feature, yes, but the tech world has expanded the concept by creating the cloud drive—that mysterious ether of digital storage that exists somewhere in the sky, an invisible vault that keeps your digital valuables safe at all times.

Strangely enough, this journey through the Stages of Joy points to heaven's own version of auto-save. If you've put your life in Christ's hands, then his Father has been accumulating every moment of goodness from your life and every priceless memory you've forgotten, and storing them in his incorruptible mind. As Digory says in *The Last Battle*, "You need not mourn over Narnia, Lucy. All of the old Narnia that mattered, all the dear creatures, have been drawn into the real Narnia through the Door."[2]

Perhaps you've forgotten that moment on your seventh birthday when you happily played in the backyard with some of the new toys you received during the party. Early dusk yellowed the sky, and the July weather filled the air with a lazy contentment. Everything was beautiful and perfect—a moment of childhood bliss. But then, to top it off, your father walked outside to you for no reason at all, gave you a hug, and told you he loved you and was proud of you. Those words of life put a glow on your face that lasted until you fell asleep that night.

But over time the glow faded and the memory with it.

God hasn't forgotten that moment. He hasn't forgotten any moment from your life. When you see him fully, exactly as he is, you will be astonished at all the spiritual treasures he's stored up for you, the things that perfectly capture who he made you to be (Col. 3:4), including all the goodness from your life that you've forgotten—the things he used to guide you up the narrow path and its many switchback trails.

I wouldn't be surprised if Jesus, when we meet him face-to-face, opens the books and allows us to see the good things from our lives with a greater clarity than when we first experienced them. Such speculation is not wild theology. It is near to the heart of the Bible. After all, Jesus said that the Father knows you so well—better than yourself, in fact—that he knows the exact number of hairs on your head (Luke 12:7). The psalmist says that all of our days are written in God's book (Psalm 139:16) and that he annotates every tear we've ever cried by storing each one in his bottle (Psalm 56:8).

We clamor to take pictures with our phones of every interesting moment and post them online, especially when we're on vacation or experiencing an important milestone, but God is already recording every minutia of goodness and storing it in his heart forever. His eyes miss nothing; they're the greatest of all cameras.

And if we let the revelation from the previous chapter sink in—that heaven is the ultimate reality, not this flimsy cardboard world—we will see that God's records of our lives have a special quality to them. It would stand to reason that God's immortal memories would be more real to our hearts than anything we experience on earth. Even the happiest triumphs of our lives have a fleeting pleasure. They come and go, and time lets us enjoy them for a few moments, but then it shoves us forward into a new sunset and a new dawn, and another night's sleep and another morning pushes us away from our greatest moments of happiness before we've had a chance to relish them. Vacations always end too early. Children always grow up too fast. Our golden days of health and youth lose their sheen just when we're getting started.

Life never feels fully formed.

But God's memories of our lives—every moment of love, grace, and goodness—are likely so rich that if we could taste his recollections of our past, they would give us a greater satisfaction and a more tangible sense of being alive than when we were actually living in those moments.

But there's another treasure he has for us. In the eternal present of heaven, the memories stay still. It won't be as our lives are now, when our happiest moments come and go in a second and evade our grasp like a bird flapping away. The memories in God's mind will retain their shape, ready for our hearts to luxuriate in them whenever we please. As long as we have intimate access to God's heart for eternity, then surely we will have unlimited access to his memories. All loving fathers relish the chance to share their memories with their children. Surely our Abba Father will do the same.

It gets even better. Heaven will have cleared the swarm of distractions that inflict us in this life. Our minds and hearts will be in a better condition to experience the memories. We will better understand the goodness that God has accumulated for us in this world, and our gladness in them will be as mighty as an ocean. We will look back on our frantic need to capture everything on camera with a sad shake of the head as we realize the obvious truth: the fleeting pleasure that we're capable of feeling in our best moments now will seem like a trickle of water compared to how we will re-experience—and relearn—those same moments in heaven.

In eternity, not only are we reunited with our lost loved ones who are in heaven, but we are also reunited with our lost lives—all of God's nuanced goodness from the many seasons of life that we have forgotten. Perhaps the apostle Paul was hinting at this when he wrote: "Set your mind on the things above, not on the things that are on earth. For you have died and your life is hidden with Christ in God. When Christ, who is our life, is revealed, then you also will be revealed with Him in glory" (Col. 3:2–4 NASB). The more we follow Paul's advice, the more that joyous, satisfying awareness of heaven's eternal accumulation will begin to sink in.

None of this is easy, of course. If we find it hard to set our minds on things above, perhaps it will encourage us to remember that all of heaven has its mind set on us. They are cheering us on. The letter to the Hebrews describes the people of faith who have gone before us as a massive "cloud of witnesses" (Heb. 12:1) that surrounds us on every side. G. K. Chesterton described this cloud as "interminable terraces full of faces looking down toward [us] intently."[3]

This topic came up when I interviewed Randy Phillips, one of the members of the Christian band Phillips, Craig & Dean. We were discussing the loss of a loved one, and he said: "When

I started picturing what Hebrews 12:1 talks about, that there's a great company around us of people that have passed over that cheer us on, I was thinking: where are my loved ones after they pass over? What happens to them? Do they see me? Do they cheer for me? What do they do? And Scripture's pretty clear about that, so I wanted to put that to music."

I then mentioned offhand the passing of my mother, and he sang a few lines from his song "Voices From The Other Side" right there over the phone. After he finished singing, his next comment stopped me in my tracks: "You miss your loved ones so much, but there's the great hope of heaven that they are more alive now than they've ever been."[4]

When this sinks in—that heaven's reality preserves the good better than anything we know on earth—a new brightness fills the House of Longing. In the midst of suffering, as we spend time with God in that House, an unshakable secret happiness fills us. We don't have to pin all our heart's peace on the accumulation of people, places, things, or memories on this earth. He records all the blessed grace and kindness that he's poured into our lives with perfect detail. Though, of course, we are not speaking of an exact revival of this old earth.

All things will be new, and the goodness from our lives that God preserves will certainly have a different quality in heaven, maybe even a different form. We can only speculate about the details, but the principle is true. Lewis explains the general truth of it this way in *The Great Divorce*, though from a slightly different approach: "I believe, to be sure, that any man who reaches heaven will find that what he abandoned (even in plucking out his right eye) has not been lost: that the kernel of what he was really seeking even in his most depraved wishes will be there, beyond expectation, waiting for him in 'the High Countries.'"[5]

The more time we spend in the secret place drawing near to God, the deeper the awareness we have of that permanence that hovers and broods over our lives and fills our cups. It's like the liquid light that Caspian drank; the revelation of heaven's permanence, and its ability to preserve and remember the good, brightens our countenance. Like the glory of a vast body of water, it gives us a sense of satisfying accumulation—of true permanence.

Window in the Skies

In the song "Window In The Skies," we get U2 at their most joyful and triumphant. With a bouncing, waltz-like rhythm, the band gives a lyrical ode to the grace of God that removes our stains, forgives our flaws, and washes our hearts clean. Their message is clear: in Christ, God has placed a window in the sky like a porthole that bridges us to heaven, and through that window he pours out his love and grace like a waterfall to anyone willing to stand under it.

But there's more to the song than just hopeful lyrics. The music, using some brilliant composition and production techniques, acts out the meaning of the words. If Bono had hummed the whole thing instead of singing his lyrics, the meaning of the song would have remained. We would have felt that waterfall pouring through the window in the skies and drenching us.

They do this by slapping the musical equivalent of window frames into the song. In fact, the first window frame appears the moment the track starts. A booming piano strike—a low bass tone as throaty as Judgment Day but somehow as bright as the pearly gates—begins the music. If you listen closely, it's not just a piano. High above in the rafters you can hear, very faintly, The Edge striking a tinny treble note in the highest register of his guitar. This combination of a high and low note striking together creates a window frame of sound—at least as far as the ear is concerned. Our brain discerns a clear boundary, a distinct shape, forming between the two notes, just as the top and bottom pieces of a window frame establish a boundary.

As soon as the two notes strike, a rush of musical information follows as Bono (and possibly The Edge too) come in on backup vocals. The vocals rise and overflow through the window formed by the two notes. This window frame appears at the beginning of each measure, and with each strike it triggers a new overflow of vocals that pour out the window.

When the verse comes in with Bono's first set of lyrics, the pattern continues. Bono waits for the two-note punch at the beginning of each measure, and then with a tumble and rush of words, he spits out his lyrics. With each new booming piano-guitar strike, it triggers another spurt of words from Bono's mouth. This cause-and-effect pattern adds to the excited sense of an I-can't-talk-about-this-fast-enough revelation; Bono is so ecstatic with the revelation of the window in the skies that he can't get the words out fast enough.

As we come closer to the chorus, The Edge adds his guitar to the musical pantomime. The cause and effect continues. As each window frame strikes, it triggers The Edge to play a descending staircase of notes. It sounds as if his guitar notes are flowing out of the window. His notes start high in the register, and then loudly flow downward to make it as obvious as possible: there's a waterfall of liquid light pouring down from the window in the skies, and The Edge is acting it out with his guitar.

Then the chorus hits. Bono belts it out. He unleashes his vocal range and allows the floodgates to open. The window pours out its water at full strength. He sings a melody that starts at the top of his register in falsetto and descends down to the earth; and he repeats this top-to-bottom melodic pattern over and over again throughout every chorus.

As the music of "Window In The Skies" acts out the meaning of its lyrics, it's impossible not to feel a stirring excitement wash over you, even if you don't understand what Bono means. The music is preaching a sermon, whether we realize it or not.

It's similar to the exhilarating rush of life that fills King Caspian when he drinks the liquid light, and it's the same rush of satisfaction that we taste deep in our souls when it finally occurs to us: because of what Jesus did on the cross for us, a divine accumulation of our lives is in progress. God is gathering all the love and goodness we've ever known and stowing it safely away in his mind.

As Jesus promises us, "My sheep hear My voice, and I know them, and they follow Me; and I give eternal life to them, and they will never perish; and no one will snatch them out of My hand" (John 10:27–28 NASB).

The Stages of Joy Playlist

4. "Window In The Skies" from U2's sessions with Rick Rubin and the album *U218 Singles*. Summary: as our understanding and awareness of the reality of heaven grows, we experience a satisfying sense of God's divine accumulation of our lives.

Scripture

"You number my wanderings;
Put my tears into Your bottle;
Are they not in Your book?"
(Ps. 56:8)

Notes for the Quest

Taking photos and storing them online has become a society-wide addiction. Every day new apps are released that add some new angle to the same objective: record and somehow possess our lives even as they pass us by. But we cannot escape the nagging feeling that our days are not truly being stowed away for safekeeping. They're slipping through our fingers like sand. But when we step into the nearness of heaven through Christ, our anxiety and depression clear. We see that we have a Father who records every tear and smile. We can release our white-knuckled grip on our days—and also on the precious people and things we've lost—and we can bury our hearts in heaven's perfect memory.

A Prayer for the Journey

Abba Father, you are perfect in every way, and you are the source of every good thing. Please don't let my heart turn the good things of life into the best things—into the supreme reasons for living. You alone are reason enough to live. Awaken my heart to the reality of your divine accumulation, and help me turn away from the addiction to earthly accumulation. In Jesus' name, amen.

More Bible Verses for the Road

Ecclesiastes 3:11; John 4:13–14; Colossians 3:4; Luke 12:7; Psalm 139:16; 56:8

CHAPTER 6

A BEAUTIFUL DAY
ON VENUS

When I wake up after Thy image,
I shall be satisfied.
– C. S. *Lewis*, Perelandra

Song to cue: "Beautiful Day"
from the album *All That You Can't Leave Behind*

The bus rumbled, creaked, and bounced through the streets of Brisbane, Australia, on a wintry night in July. (I write "wintry" because the seasons are reversed in Australia; their winters happen during North America's summer months.) I tried, with a slight measure of success, to hold a book steady. But my eyes still fought to catch the words bouncing along with the bus. Finally, I focused on the following sentences: "The roots of our hearts have grown down into things, and we dare not pull up one rootlet lest we die. Things have become necessary to us, a development never originally intended. God's gifts now take the place of God, and the whole course of nature is upset by the monstrous substitution."[1]

The book was *The Pursuit of God* by A.W. Tozer, published

in 1948, and those words came from chapter 2, "The Blessedness of Possessing Nothing." (And, just to be clear, it's not about taking a vow of poverty.) That little book altered the course of my life, and it became deeply connected to what C. S. Lewis' books and U2's music would do later. Tozer describes how a deep hunger for God—a hunger that flows with the same Longing found in Joy—will always rip out the roots of our hearts from this world's soil. When that happens, the heart no longer clings to any earthly thing. We cease to possess anything, no matter how much we have.

As that truth sank into my spirit that night, I felt a measure of kinship with Tozer. He wrote *The Pursuit of God* with a pencil on a train, and I read it on a bus. We were both in transit, grabbing hold of words the best we could. And we were both sensing the same peculiarity of this life: *everything* is in transit. As I briefly mentioned in the previous chapter, nothing in this world stays still long enough to satisfy our Longing. Inconsolable motion buzzes everywhere and hums in the background of every sound, color, and smell around us.

Years after that bus ride, when dark seasons of suffering came, my whole life rocked with this sense of transit. Whether I sat at home alone or stood in a church with a crowd of people, my existence felt like a moving train. Life was no longer settled. The roots had broken loose from the soil.

In the previous chapter, we saw how the House of Longing brings a comforting revelation about heaven's reality—its accumulation of goodness and permanence. But the House of Longing also takes us to an operating room, and it has a clear medical objective: to obliterate any degree of possessiveness from our hearts. God gives us a sense of heaven's permanence for one purpose: to teach our hearts to let go—to finally get the truth in our hearts, not just in our heads, that nothing we have really belongs to us. The feeling that we possess anything in this wispy world-in-transit is a grand illusion. The Scriptures don't parse words: "Naked I came from my mother's womb, and naked I shall return there" (Job 1:21 NASB).

As we get further into the House of Longing, we discover something else: the House itself is moving. It's not moored to the ground—at least not to this world's ground. The House is more like the house carried away by the balloons in the movie *Up*. The whole structure defies gravity and moves toward the sky. And the more it fills us with an awareness of heaven as ultimate reality, the more it asks us to let go of everything on earth.

This does not always mean we take a vow of poverty, cut off our relationships, sell our homes, and move to a monastery; it simply means we no longer possess those things, people, and places in our hearts. We stop seeing them as ours. We relinquish our claim of ownership, and we don't cling to the good things of life as the best things.

We don't let the roots of our identity grow down into them.

Having Things Over Again (and Again)

A trip to the planet Venus provides one of the best illustrations of the truths above, especially if you travel with a man named Elwin Ransom. I'm referring, of course, to the Space Trilogy by C. S. Lewis, his three marvelous science fiction books (*Out of the Silent Planet*, *Perelandra*, and *That Hideous Strength*) published between 1938 and 1945.

In the first two books, Ransom, a philologist and professor

modeled after Lewis' friend J. R. R. Tolkien,[2] is swept up into a secret journey to Mars and Venus. Lewis himself is a character in the story and the narrator. In Book 2, *Perelandra*, Ransom travels alone in a coffin-like space capsule and lands in the oceans of Venus, the planet that the non-human inhabitants of the solar system call Perelandra, which is an unspoiled paradise.

Ransom catches his breath as he beholds the planet's golden sky and emerald sea: "The very names of green and gold, which he used perforce in describing the scene, are too harsh for the tenderness, the muted iridescence, of that warm, maternal, delicately gorgeous world. It was mild to look upon as evening, warm like summer noon, gentle and winning like early dawn."[3]

Ransom discovers that most of the landmasses on the planet float on the surface of the sea. In order to accomplish anything, he must relearn how to walk because the ground is constantly moving—like learning to walk on a ship during a storm, except with the added challenge of malleable earth that conforms to the shifting contours of the ocean's swells.

After learning to walk on the fast-changing, unpredictable ground, he tastes some of the food—a gourd hanging from a tree. The intense pleasure of it overwhelms him, and he wants more, lots more. On earth, he would not have hesitated to satisfy the craving and gorge himself. But something about the virgin paradise of Perelandra, something in the mood and spirit of the strange planet, restrains him:

> His reason, or what we commonly take to be reason in our own world, was all in favor of tasting this miracle again.... Yet something seemed opposed to this "reason."

It is difficult to suppose that this opposition came from desire, for what desire would turn from so much deliciousness? But for whatever cause, it appeared to him better not to taste again. Perhaps the experience had been so complete that repetition would be a vulgarity—like asking to hear the same symphony twice in a day.[4]

Later in the story, Ransom notes this feeling of restraint again when he encounters bubbles that hang from trees. When he walks through one, the bubble pops and showers him with delightful, soothing sensations. He sees a long line of the bubbles, and he thinks about running through them greedily to make them pop over his head all at once, but then a thought enters his mind: "This itch to have things over again, as if life were a film that could be unrolled twice or even made to work backward…was it possibly the root of all evil? No: of course the love of money was called that. But money itself—perhaps one valued it chiefly as a defense against chance, a security for being able to have things over again, a means of arresting the unrolling of the film."[5]

As Ransom learns later in his journey, it was not just his virtue that restrained his possessive need for the gourd and the bubbles. The planet itself—or, more accurately, the Presence of One who inhabited it—helped Ransom. In a similar way, in our quest through the Stages of Joy, the House of Longing works to loosen our roots that have grown down into this world.

But it's not always pleasant.

This unmooring of our roots can be unsettling. Throughout our whole lives we have learned to walk on fixed land, but now we're staggering across a strange, undulating terrain that moves as wildly and fluidly as the surface of the ocean.

We must relearn how to walk.

We navigate a tricky in-between ground where a part of us lives in the House of Longing, enthralled with the realness of heaven, while another part of us keeps its roots tangled in the passions and pursuits of this world.

The more time we spend in the secret place of the House of Longing—and the more we apply what we learn there to our worldly interactions—the easier it will be for us to do what Ransom did: to let go of our grabby compulsion to "have things over again," to possess all of this life's happiness with a white-knuckled grip.

But when our hearts finally relinquish ownership, something surprising happens: we discover that losing everything voluntarily—in other words, letting the hand of God unearth our shivering rootlets from the soil and transplant us—actually results in the most beautiful day we have ever had.

After We Lose Everything

Sometime around the year 2000, after Bono finished his Jubilee 2000 campaign to erase third-world debt, he wrote a song about a man who loses everything but still finds joy.[6] This became the massive hit "Beautiful Day," which has since inundated the conscience of Western culture. Biblical imagery, particularly from the Genesis account of Noah and the flood, saturate the song. While scores of music journalists, critics, and commenters on fan sites have analyzed this song's lyrical meaning, not much has been said about its musical meaning.

With "Beautiful Day," the goldmine of meaning lies in the beat—in the song's soaring schematic of boom-boom-boom. And that's exactly how the song begins: a heart-like thump-thump of a Euro kick drum put together by producer Brian Eno,[7] along with the murmuration of synth chords floating behind. This launches "Beautiful Day" into a steady, brisk walk—a driving, levelheaded tempo with a tinge of urgency like the hurried pace of a New Yorker on the sidewalk. (We'll call this rhythm the New Yorker's Walk.)

When the chorus hits, as Bono shouts the song's title, the whole song is thrown off-balance. The driving rhythm of the New Yorker's Walk vanishes, and an off-kilter upheaval takes its place. The song suddenly feels like a ship at sea when it lurches on a wave and everyone on deck staggers to one side of the boat. U2 achieves this by using dotted rhythms—notes with rhythmic values that hold their note and suspend in space for a moment instead of striking every beat of the song.

This technique makes it harder for the ear to pick out every beat of a tempo, and it adds a funky sense of syncopation, as if a businessperson walking with fast, determined steps down the avenue had suddenly halted and started dancing to James Brown, hopping a little or sliding here. An odd analogy, perhaps, but that's how dramatic the rhythmic contrast is between the verses and the chorus in "Beautiful Day."

The contrast—on one side is the even, driving New Yorker's Walk, and on the other is the funky, off-balance syncopation—shows us what Joy does. It disrupts our sense of balance. The further we go on this journey, the more we will find ourselves treading on the islands of Perelandra, the ground that shifts with every rise and fall of the ocean. Everything is in transit, including our hearts.

But that's a good thing.

The One who has hurtled us forward with Deep Longing has a glorious destination in mind. If we surrender, if we learn to let go of our treasures instead of clinging to them, our sense of heaven's permanence and accumulation will grow. As Jesus said, "If you cling to your life, you will lose it; but if you give up your life for me, you will find it" (Matt 10:39 NLT).

For Ransom, learning to walk on Perelandra's thin, flexible islands that moved with the contours of the ocean was like "learning to walk on water itself."[8] And as it was true for Ransom (and the apostle Peter), so it is true for us: the sooner we learn to walk on water, the better.

The Stages of Joy Playlist

5. "Beautiful Day" from the album *All That You Can't Leave Behind*. Summary: The House of Longing comforts us with an awareness of heaven, but it is also in motion; it keeps us in transit and uproots our hearts from the comforts of this world.

Scripture

"He who finds his life will lose it, and he who loses his life for My sake will find it" (Matt. 10:37–39).

Notes for the Quest

The gospel confounds the world. The world sees happiness in terms of material possessions and security—of having everything you need. And this is not some pagan worldview. Western Christianity has pursued all the trappings of earthly happiness as if its life depends on it—especially the wholesome trappings of home and hearth. But our lives don't depend on earthly happiness. That is one of the most fundamentally challenging messages of the Bible—not just for unbelievers, but for believers too. When we lose everything, it is not the end of the story. Christ specializes in building palaces from ruins. The more we see this and accept it, the easier it becomes to trust him and to step off the fixed land of earthly needs and walk on water.

A Prayer for the Journey

Abba Father, I confess that sometimes your Word terrifies me. It commands me to do frightening things such as walk on water in the middle of a storm. It says that I should not try to save my life and live for myself but lose my life for your sake. Forgive me for all the times I've quietly refused to do this. Give me a new heart, a soft heart, that is willing to follow you anywhere, that trusts you no matter what, and that feels the hope we have in you, even when everything falls apart. In Jesus' name, amen.

More Bible Verses for the Road

Job 1:21; Matthew 10:37–39

PART III

ZOOROPA:
HOW OUR SECULAR AGE
POISONS JOY AND GRIEF

WHERE WE ARE ON THE MAP:
A SUMMARY OF PART II

- As we spend time in the House of Longing, heaven invades, and we fix our attention on the true reality that lies beyond the blinding lights of this world.

- As our understanding and awareness of the reality of heaven grows, we experience a satisfying sense of God's divine accumulation of our lives.

- The House of Longing comforts us with an awareness of heaven, but it is also in motion; it keeps us in transit and uproots our hearts from the comforts of this world. And when sorrows push us off fixed land, Christ teaches us how to walk on water.

CHAPTER 7

WINTER IN
THE AGE OF ZOOROPA

They say an unhappy man wants distractions—
something to take him out of himself.
– C. S. *Lewis*, A Grief Observed

Song to cue: "Zooropa"
from the album *Zooropa*

I f you were there when it happened, remembering it
might feel like recalling the strangest dream.

Walls of giant television screens as tall as a building flicker
to life with static. Small German cars called Trabants—tiny
1957 Communist-made cars rated among the fifty worst cars
in history[1]—hang from cranes and shine on you with their
headlights. A strange man with bulbous, oversized black sun-
glasses shaped like the eyes of a fly—part lounge singer, part
rent-a-rock-star, part stage actor in costume—creeps across
the face of the flickering screens. Later he is channel surfing
on the giant televisions and making prank phone calls to the
White House.

Random advertising messages and popular slogans blink

everywhere on the giant TVs: "text, sayings, truisms, untruisms, oxymorons, soothsayings, etc., all blasted at high speed, just fast enough so it's impossible to actually read what's being said."[2] Broadcast towers surround the screens, so tall that blinking lights have been placed at the top of them to warn aircraft of their presence.[3] The cranes, screens, and towers resemble the "techno-future cityscapes" of the film *Blade Runner* and the surreal cities of cyberpunk fiction.[4]

Other oddities appear on the building-sized screens: a cleverly spliced video of George Bush Sr. rapping to the song "We Will Rock You" by Queen; a cutout of a woman's head spinning like a vinyl record; and then, just when you thought the dream couldn't get stranger, a mirror-ball appears in one of the hanging Trabants and a member of ABBA stands below it to sing a duet with the man wearing the bulbous shades.

While everything above might sound like the dream of a Surrealist painter, all of it happened during ZooTV, U2's record-breaking tour that supported the albums *Achtung Baby* and *Zooropa* from February 1992 to December 1993.[5]

ZooTV, on the surface, might have seemed absurd in its spectacle, but it presented a sharp critique of our culture, especially the world's media oversaturation and information overload. Eerily, it foretold the onslaught of our current screen age—our world's frightening addiction to mobile devices, the Internet, and social media. As Michael Bracewell writes in the book *U2 Show*: "Loosely, ZooTV…could be said to articulate statements about the postmodern world—describing that world back to itself as a perilous pleasure dome of seemingly infinite images and information, the accelerated accumulation of which might seem to threaten our perceptions, free will and fundamental human feelings."[6]

If the modern world can threaten our "perceptions, free will and fundamental human feelings," then it can surely threaten, if not completely obliterate, the journey of Joy described in this book.

How?

One attack comes through distraction—loads and loads of shallow, flittering distraction.

The Gale Force Cross-Pressures of the Secular Age

It's no secret that our secular age, far from being an age of total unbelief—as if religion had died out decades ago—is an age of intense "cross-pressures,"[7] as Christian philosopher Charles Taylor coined it. Two great fronts of weather collide in the secular age, and no one, whether religious or non-religious, can escape these cross-pressures.

On one side of this massive collision is the idea of immanence, the sense that the material world is all there is; therefore, we should put all of our hopes in this life and not live with eternity in mind. Many of those who have argued zealously for immanence have organized their beliefs into secular humanism and the New Atheism, which say that human reason is the ultimate arbitrator of truth and the sole creator of meaning, because, as the narrative goes, the material universe is all there is.

Taylor, in his book *A Secular Age*, uses the term "exclusive humanism" to describe this mind-set. Christian philosopher James K. A. Smith, in his book *How (Not) to Be Secular: Reading Charles Taylor*, defines exclusive humanism this way:

"A worldview or social imaginary that is able to account for meaning and significance without any appeal to the divine or transcendence."[8]

On the other side is transcendence, the general belief that there's something more than this material world, and that life exists after death. We should therefore live with eternity in mind and seek God now. (Christianity, interestingly, teaches that God has sought us by choosing to be born into the human race to live among us, to give us a tangible, relatable, touchable picture of his divinity, and to suffer and die for us. Joan Osborne's 1995 song, "One of Us," was on to something: God *was* one of us.)

Most of humanity stands in the middle of these weather fronts of immanence and transcendence, and, as far as I can tell, most of us don't run very hard in either direction. (I've certainly been guilty of the middle road myself.) In the West, most secularists are not hardcore, outspoken atheists trying to convert religious people to their views, and most Christians aren't impassioned evangelists standing on street corners preaching the gospel.

Especially in prosperous societies, like Laodicea with its "lukewarm" Christians (Rev. 3:14–22), it's easy to look for a comfortable nook, an insulated shelter, where neither the winds of immanence nor transcendence push too hard. We might believe in heaven and in the gospel, but in the day-to-day focus of our lives, immanence consumes us, especially when we throw the digital age into the mix.

Suddenly we find ourselves neck deep in ZooTV. The technology we consume begins to loom over us like the larger-than-life screens of U2's show. Like the madness of ZooTV, our coping mechanisms, comfort foods, and addictions distract us from the Deep Longing—from transcendence and the cross-pressures. If we're in the midst of grief, the desire to numb the pain and push reality away with a flood of distractions becomes even stronger. But in the midst of all the noise and screens, our emptiness and pain quietly grows.

Charles Taylor describes the emptiness of our ZooTV environment this way: "Some people feel a terrible flatness in the everyday, and this experience has been identified particularly with commercial, industrial, or consumer society. [We] feel emptiness of the repeated, accelerating cycle of desire and fulfillment, in consumer culture; the cardboard quality of bright supermarkets, or neat row housing in a clean suburb."[9]

James K. A. Smith describes our coping mechanisms: "The dissatisfaction and emptiness can propel a return to transcendence [to God and belief in eternity]. But often—and perhaps more often than not now?—the 'cure' to this nagging pressure of absence is sought within immanence [earthly pursuits and distractions], and it is this quest that generates the nova effect, looking for love/meaning/significance/quasi 'transcendence' within the immanent order."[10]

Our secular age, in other words, has exploded into a supernova of distractions as we run for cover from the intense cross-pressures. And most of it has now been corralled into one place.

The Internet.

Our Virtual Lives Versus Joy

A man once made a stunning prediction about the future, though most of us have never heard of it. This is what he wrote:

"Thought will spread across the world with the rapidity of light, instantly conceived, instantly written, instantly understood. It will blanket the earth from one pole to the other—sudden, instantaneous, burning with the fervor of the soul from which it burst forth. This will be the reign of the human word in all its plenitude. Thought will not have time to ripen, to accumulate into the form of a book—the book will arrive too late."[11]

It's a rather dramatic, poetic description of the Internet, right?

Nope. Actually, Alphonse de Lamartine, a French poet and politician, wrote it in 1831.

He was writing about the newspaper, and thought the new medium would be the doom of books. If Lamartine had such dramatic thoughts about the newspaper, he might have lost his mind if he had known what was coming in the 1990s and early 2000s. If there ever was an age in which thoughts are spouted off to the world before they have time to ripen, this is it. And we have swallowed this pill before knowing any of the side effects.

In fact, Nicholas Carr, former executive editor of the *Harvard Business Review*, wrote a book called *The Shallows: What the Internet is Doing to Our Brains*. He made a sobering assessment: Western civilization is losing its ability to concentrate—on anything. Some people might shrug at that, but the implications are unsettling, as noted by NPR in its review of Carr's book:

> Deep reading, which requires "sustained, unbroken attention to a single, static object," has for ages allowed people to make "their own associations, draw their own inferences and analogies, foster their own ideas." The Internet

works against this, Carr writes. "Dozens of studies by psychologists, neurobiologists, educators and Web designers point to the same conclusion: when we go online, we enter an environment that promotes cursory reading, hurried and distracted thinking, and superficial learning." Sure, deep reading is possible, but that's not the kind of reading "the technology encourages and rewards."[12]

NPR zeroes in on something that U2 with its ZooTV tour and its albums *Achtung Baby*, *Zooropa*, and *Pop*, had already predicted twenty years ago. The sensory overload of our age is causing so much distraction that it's numbing our brains:

With *The Shallows*, Carr attempts to snap us out of the hypnotic pull of our iPhones, laptops, and desktops. He reveals why we're suddenly having a hard time focusing at length on any given thing, and why we compulsively check our e-mail accounts and Twitter feeds and never seem to be able to get our work done. (It's because we've been abusing our brains.) He wants us to value wisdom over knowledge, and to use new technology intelligently. "We shouldn't allow the glories of technology to blind our inner watchdog to the possibility that we've numbed an essential part of our self," Carr pleads. It remains to be seen if he's shouted down or listened to.[13]

When we gorge ourselves on our digital drugs, the distractions of the secular age swoop in. And in the sharp pain of grief, we welcome the numbness. But there is an unintended consequence: Joy is numbed too. Our Deep Longing vanishes beneath the ice.

Zooropa: Freezing Nights and Bright Lights

In U2's 1993 album *Zooropa*, the most obvious song that could apply to this chaos would be "Numb," because of its lyrical content and the way The Edge speak-sings the words in a monotone voice, acting out the numbness described in the song with a deadpan singing style. The song summarizes the message of ZooTV: our modern world's hyperactive messaging bombards us every day with advertising, pop psychology, recycled meme-like slogans, and 24/7 news cycles, and it is making us numb, as David Carr concluded.

If "Numb" describes the problem, then the song "Zooropa" describes the solution. In its unique sonic landscape, we find a parable that leads us out of the numbness of the secular age. It begins with The Edge's guitar pedal.

After the song's chaotic ZooTV-esque intro, with washes of static and beeps and garbled voices looping over digital fuzz like the sound of traffic in a futuristic cityscape, the guitar comes in. It sounds almost like a human voice, distorted and singing—the *wah wah* of Charlie Brown's teacher fed through the robo-voicebox of R2D2 who's singing a Gregorian chant in a reverb-washed cathedral. (Guitars can do very strange things.)

The heart of this peculiar sound is The Edge's wah pedal and the science behind wah pedals in general. The wah pedal uses a trick in sound engineering called low-pass filtering (or, in some cases, band-pass filtering).[14] It functions like a bouncer at a club, letting some people in but keeping others out. If you play a guitar through a low-pass filter, the bouncer lets in the frequencies of your guitar tone below a certain demarcation point. Any frequencies above that point are kept out. With a wah pedal, you can control the precise location of this demarcation point, either by depressing the pedal with your foot or by setting the knobs on the pedal.

But The Edge doesn't stop with the wah pedal. He then multiplies his filtered tone by sending it through two delay pedals[15], devices that digitally repeat the notes with cascades of echoes. It sounds as if the notes are splitting into pieces on an atomic level and bouncing around a cathedral ceiling like a thousand sonic pinballs. It overwhelms the stereo field.

The Edge's guitar multiplies into scores of echoing moonshots, and he becomes the primary voice of the song, even overshadowing Bono. In the first minute or two, this guitar sound rises slowly over the chaotic noise of ZooTV, as if to say, "My guitar is here to overcome ZooTV and push the chaos aside. Let the real song begin." The rest of the band doesn't even come in until the guitar's conquering fade-in is complete. It's as if U2 could not play the song until the noise dragon of ZooTV was slain by the guitar.

The protagonist of the song, the character whom Bono assumes with his lyrics, is a person who has no direction or absolute truth—no religion or any sense of what things are. (Though, interestingly, when I saw U2 play at Angel Stadium in Anaheim, California, for the 360 Tour, they skipped the stanza in "Zooropa" that talks about having no religion.)

During the 1990s, Bono would often assume other characters as a kind of satire and exposé. It was an artful way of holding our modern culture up for examination and critique—much the same way that C. S. Lewis assumed the voice of a demon in *The Screwtape Letters* to expose the deceptive strategies of the Enemy. (In fact, the subversive tactics of *The Screwtape Letters*, one of Bono's favorite books, inspired Bono's on-stage personas The Fly and Macphisto during the ZooTV tour.)[16]

In "Zooropa," as the song structure unfolds, The Edge's wah-wah guitar continues to lead the way to deliverance from ZooTV. The more it plays and repeats its primary themes, the more liberated the song becomes—getting louder, higher, and more elated in its sonic range and rhythm—as if the guitar is conducting an exorcism of the protagonist.

Then suddenly, at the height of the bridge between 4:44 and 5:03, when the band is playing its loudest and Bono is triumphantly singing at the top of his range, the protagonist in the lyric escapes from the underground and reaches the surface streets—stepping out from the dark, muggy subway tunnels and into the bright air on a chilly night.

In a figurative sense, we need to follow him. We need to follow the character in "Zooropa," with his spinning neon wah-wah beacon, out of the subway. This boils down to a reminder of something we all know: there must be times when we leave the zoo and find sanctuary and solitude—not just physical solitude, but digital solitude, cutting the umbilical cord between our minds and the zoo on the Internet.

If we don't, we might disappear and dissolve completely into what Charles Taylor called the "nova effect"[17]—an explosion of interests and fixations that comes whenever a society rejects heaven's eternal perspective, replaces it with the world's immanence, declares that this life is all we have, but then desperately tries to recreate heaven's transcendence using non-heavenly, material resources. We look for quasi-transcendence "within the imminent order," as Smith wrote. This mimicry of heaven's transcendence, without ever acknowledging or surrendering to God, is what creates the spiritual madness of ZooTV.

For many others, however, the digital age provides a welcome distraction from the whole question, from the cross-pressures of belief and non-belief. Instead of dealing with the persistent claims of immanence (that there is no God who keeps us accountable, and life is ultimately meaningless) and transcendence (that there is a God and he created life and fills it with meaning), our culture just shoves both voices as far away as possible and lives in a strange in-between state that samples fruits from each side.

We taste our transcendence in small, comfortable doses, but just enough without having to go all in. And then we gorge on immanence, and become fixated on our earthly goals in the here and now as if eternity and heaven are irrelevant. Both Christians and non-Christians do this in equal measure. (I've been guilty of it too at times.)

If we're Christians skirting the cross-pressures, we don't buy into full-blown transcendence. We don't throw ourselves wholeheartedly into the mission that Christ has given us, and we don't fully embrace the delayed gratification of spiritual riches. If we're atheists, we don't buy into full-blown immanence. We don't really live each day as if the cosmos were a godless, meaningless vacuum and life is purposeless, even if that is the logical conclusion of our worldview. The modern age lives in denial of both heaven and oblivion. We've become half-creatures with lukewarm blood, neither hot nor cold.

But our attempts to push the cross-pressures away will always backfire. Our middle ground invites even stronger crosswinds, and the cycle repeats: we flee into screens, things, and people to escape. Meanwhile, our progress through the Stages of Joy comes to a halt. Unless we face these headwinds and stop taking refuge in our distractions and comforts, unless we limit our dependence on the digital age, we will become trapped in the vicious cycle.

It might seem like an odd analogy, but The Edge's wah pedal, and the way it functions in "Zooropa," acts out a parable for us. It shows us a clear picture of something—a precise, intentional limiting of information. With the slightest movement of the pedal, the musician can control which frequencies are allowed to flow out of the amplifier. Do we exert control over the flow of digital distraction in our lives? Do we place precise limits on it like a low-pass filter? Or does ZooTV's digital supernova control our lives?

Sadly, we are slow to give up our beloved distractions or accept any kind of boundaries. Our Western individualism doesn't help matters. The West lives in what Charles Taylor calls the age of "expressive individualism." Emerging from the Romantic expressivism of the late eighteenth century, as James K. A. Smith notes, this mind-set is an understanding "that each one of us has his or her own way of realizing our humanity, and that we are called to live that out ('express' it) rather than conform to models imposed by others, especially institutions."[18]

In other words, the modern age does not take kindly to

limits of any kind—especially limits imposed by any perceived authority. In fact, our modern instinct to defy authority and rule with absolute power over what we see as our domain is reminiscent of someone whom the readers of *The Chronicles of Narnia* know very well.

The White Witch, Deep Magic, and Yielding to Aslan

In C. S. Lewis' most celebrated work of fiction, *The Chronicles of Narnia: The Lion, the Witch and the Wardrobe*, we meet his most famous villain, the White Witch. She has conquered Narnia and assumed the title of monarch, and in her cruelty she has frozen Narnia with a brutal winter. When the faun Tumnus meets Lucy near the lamppost, he says, "Why, it is she that has got all Narnia under her thumb. It's she that makes it always winter. Always winter and never Christmas; think of that!"[19]

Later in the story, the White Witch thinks she has finally triumphed when she uses the laws of the Deep Magic to kill Aslan, the great Lion and the rightful ruler of Narnia. But when Aslan rises from the dead, Lucy cannot believe her eyes, and she and Susan ask him what it all means:

"It means," said Aslan, "that though the Witch knew the Deep Magic, there is a magic deeper still which she did not know. Her knowledge goes back only to the dawn of time. But if she could have looked a little further back, into the stillness and the darkness before Time dawned, she would have read there a different incantation. She would have known that when a willing victim who had committed no treachery was killed in a traitor's stead, the

Table would crack and Death itself would start working backward. And now—"

"Oh yes. Now?" said Lucy, jumping up and clapping her hands.

"Oh, children," said the Lion, "I feel my strength coming back to me. Oh, children, catch me if you can!" He stood for a second, his eyes very bright, his limbs quivering, lashing himself with his tail. Then he made a leap high over their heads and landed on the other side of the Table.[20]

Like the White Witch, we think we know better than anyone else what's best for us, and we assume that we have all the facts straight. As a culture we've become fiercely prideful. We want total control and refuse any limits. We have the Internet and the wonders of the screen age at our fingertips, and we think we understand the Deep Magic. Even if we don't, Siri will tell us, and there's probably an app for it.

But there is a deeper magic (in the Narnian sense, not the occultic) waiting for us in the stillness. It waits in the darkness of a quiet room where nothing can distract us from seeking God—if we would just spend time with him.

At a time in my life when I desperately needed to spend more time in prayer, my dad wrote me a letter and shared this quote from D. L. Moody: "If you have so much business to attend to that you have no time to pray, depend upon it, you have more business on hand than God ever intended you should have."[21]

If we ignore D. L. Moody's advice and let ZooTV have reign over our lives, the numbness that U2 warned about will conquer everything, including our ability to grieve properly. The journey to Joy will stop. Even worse, we might believe in Christ and the reality of heaven, but our constant string of distractions will add up to a passive unbelief—a paralysis of faith and a lazy inaction as destructive as if we were actively opposing heaven and embracing immanence.

The way out is to welcome Christ's benevolent monarchy, to yield to the Deep Magic, and to bow to Aslan's Spring—to surrender the comings and goings of our lives to the Deep Longing that calls us away from immanence. If we do, we will "feel our strength coming back to us," as Aslan did, and we will be back on the journey through Joy.

But we might need to do something drastic.

We might need time away from our computers, mobile devices, social media networks, e-mails, Netflix binges, movie theaters, Snapchat videos, and Periscope streaming sessions. It might be a fight sometimes—it could be costly if our careers rely on them—but it's worth the sacrifice. Will we spend serious time with the One who knows the number of hairs on our heads? Will we accept his limitations and rule over our schedules?

If we do, something glorious will happen. The snow and the numbness will begin to melt.

The Stages of Joy Playlist

6. "Zooropa" from the album *Zooropa*. Summary: our digital age threatens to numb our hearts, stop our journey through Joy, and poison how we grieve. To overcome it, we must allow Christ's rule to create boundaries in our lives.

Scripture

"The one I love calls to me:
[The Bridegroom-King]
Arise, my dearest. Hurry, my darling.
Come along with me!
I have come as you have asked
to draw you to my heart and lead you out.
For now is the time, my beautiful one.
The season has changed,
the bondage of your barren winter has ended,
and the season of hiding is over and gone.
The rains have soaked the earth
and left it bright with blossoming flowers.
The season for singing and pruning the vines has arrived."
(Song of Songs 2:10–12 TPT)[22]

Notes for the Quest

Spending time with God is not a works-based system of rules. It is not a cold, lifeless to-do list that we maintain to feel a sense of righteous self-satisfaction. It is a warm relationship. That being said, it takes discipline and practical strategies to build the habit. Try these ideas if you're having trouble with your time management strategy:

- Begin with small goals. If you don't have a habit of spending time with God each day, take small steps. Begin with fifteen minutes a day, and then gradually increase your time as your habit takes hold. Aim for an hour each day as a long-term goal.

- Be creative with your location. If your home environment offers no easy place where you can pray uninterrupted, use your car during lunch breaks while you're at work. Ask your local church if you could use a room in their facility. Consider finding an outdoor location—a park or hiking trail—that offers quiet natural beauty.
- Be intentional about unplugging from the digital world and communicating with others ahead of time. If you rely on the Internet for work, notify colleagues that you will be unavailable during the time frame of your vacation from technology. Set up a vacation responder auto-reply in your e-mail to notify others of your absence from digital communications and when you will be available again to respond.

A Prayer for the Journey

Abba Father, I ask for wisdom in my pursuit of you. Show me the path forward out of the chaos of the modern world's distractions. Give me the desire and determination needed to put my relationship with you first above all other things. And I ask for the wisdom and discipline to carry out a successful strategy—a plan that will build a clear boundary around my time with you. Help me to surrender to your voice, and help my heart to trust you and yield to the healthy limits that you want to place in my life. In Jesus' name, amen.

More Bible Verses for the Road

Revelation 3:14–22

CHAPTER 8

THEY HAVE PULLED DOWN DEEP HEAVEN ON THEIR HEADS

The world is charged with the grandeur of God.
– Gerard Manley Hopkins

Song to cue: "If God Will Send His Angels"
from the album *Pop*

It is true, we must escape the feedback loop of ZooTV, but that escape is only the first step. Simply unplugging is not enough. We can't just reduce the noise and static in our lives. This is not only a process of negation, of eliminating something bad; it is also a process of addition, of putting something good back in.

We need a treasure hunt.

We need to rediscover a precious jewel that was lost to Western civilization centuries ago. If we are going to push through the lukewarm disenchantment of our world, we must understand how we came to this point and how our culture's ZooTV became possible in the first place.

But you should be warned: the origin story of our secular age is surprising, if not a little horrifying.

A Fatal Disenchantment: The Proud Cult of Scientism

The term "disenchantment" in our culture could be defined this way: big chunks of society no longer believe in a connection to a supernatural reality beyond what we can see and hear. When we survey the world around us, we no longer see any inherent spiritual meaning or value embedded there by God. The universe is cold machination—soulless clockwork.

Disenchantment is also a sign of something else: the elevation of human reason to the highest throne of authority and hope. Our relationship with science is a prime case. Scientific inquiry is a wonderful thing if it keeps a humble heart—if it knows its limits in the search for truth and collaborates with, not dominates or misuses, the other methods of inquiry such as philosophy and theology.

But long before any of us were born, something new emerged from culture. A philosophical outgrowth from science called "scientism" roared to life in the late 1800s and early 1900s, especially in C. S. Lewis' day. According to its formal definition, scientism claims that "science alone can render truth about the world and reality....Scientism sees it necessary to do away with most, if not all, metaphysical, philosophical, and religious claims."[1]

Scientism became the primary weapon that exclusive humanists used to thrust disenchantment through the heart of the West—and many of them still use it today. C. S. Lewis fought against it mercilessly in his writings.

Scientism, among other things, coldly reduces all human

experience to the lifeless jargon of scientific language. For example, when a biologist tells two people who are desperately in love—two souls who believe they share a spiritual connection that transcends mere biology—that their love is nothing more than chemical reactions in their brains, it disenchants the two lovers. It strips the transcendent meaning from their relationship and reduces it to a study of two organisms interacting beneath a microscope.

Since the early 1900s, scientism has seeped into the largest institutions of Western culture. Its direct and indirect influence can be felt everywhere, from the serious lectures of a college classroom to the silly scenes of a comedy. Sure, it's hard not to laugh in the film *Nacho Libre* when Jack Black's Christian character Nacho tries to surprise baptize his friend Esqueleto. And when the two argue about their beliefs, Esqueleto proclaims, "I only believe in science!" Yet that is the true response of millions in Western society.

Even if we are Christians who have an unshakable belief in the supernatural, the constant pressure of scientism's influence in our culture can suck the vibrancy out of our relationship with God. It can quietly sever the grandeur of God from our perception of the world and the relationships around us.

To reconnect what has been severed, we must push through layers of unspoken, unchallenged presuppositions that our ancestors piled up long before we were born. We must reject, to some degree, the label of "darkness" that has been plastered sloppily across medieval history.

For example, Petrarch, known as the father of humanism, created the term "Dark Ages."[2] The Enlightenment crowd seized upon the term as if they were saying, "Nothing to see here, folks. Move along." But we do need to see what was there—to look beyond the stereotypes and grievances that modern culture has slathered all over medieval thought. We need to see for ourselves some of the treasures that humanity has lost in its rush to become secular.

There's one particular treasure that we desperately need back again—at least a modified version of it. We have lost what philosopher Hans Boersma calls the "sacramental mindset."[3] A sacrament, according to its dictionary definition, is an outward "sign or symbol of a spiritual reality."[4] In his book *Heavenly Participation: The Weaving of a Sacramental Tapestry*, Boersma's "sacramental mindset" refers to the belief that the universe is sacramental by nature—meaning everything that God has made, from the human eye to a distant galaxy, functions in some degree as a sign or symbol of a spiritual reality.

For example, I believe that the laws that govern music can function as a symbol of spiritual reality. I believe that God, when he designed the universe, hid Easter eggs of revelation about himself in creation. This is why I look for theological truths in the physics of sound and the mechanics of music theory.

Most of Western civilization once had this mind-set. The average person used to see the world charged with the grandeur of God, as if God had hidden little treasures of meaning in every facet of the universe. This viewpoint was so common that it was taken for granted. The medieval mind had a rich, intuitive grasp of Romans 1:20: "For since the creation of the world God's invisible qualities—his eternal power and divine nature—have been clearly seen, being understood from what has been made" (NIV).

Charles Taylor's philosophical masterpiece *A Secular Age*, as summarized by James K. A. Smith, says this about the medieval Christian view: "The natural world was constituted as a cosmos that functioned semiotically, as a sign that pointed beyond itself, to what was more than nature....In sum, people lived in an enchanted world, a world 'charged' with presences, that was open and vulnerable, not closed and self-sufficient."[5]

This enchantment, the habit of seeing creation as a sign pointing to God, is a necessity for experiencing Joy. Without it, Joy loses its traction. The painfully enormous bliss it brings—its inconsolable longing that moves us to a higher pilgrimage in the spirit—can't take hold of us. It becomes diffuse, vapid, and toothless. It might collide with our hearts, but like a glancing arrow it can't sink in.

Boersma writes that our secular age, including many of its Christian movements, has laid waste to the sacramental mind-set: "once modernity abandoned a participatory or sacramental view of reality, the created order became unmoored from its origin in God, and the material cosmos began its precarious drift on the flux of nihilistic waves."[6] Once the Western world lost this sacramental mind-set—an outlook that suffered its first serious wound in the late Middle Ages, between 1200 and 1500—it opened the door to our secular age of disenchantment.

Most of us think the secular age is a recent trend—perhaps something beginning with the cultural revolution of the 1960s, but this is a serious miscalculation. The rise of the secular age began centuries ago; 1960 was merely the public grand opening of a project that had begun hundreds of years prior. Until we understand this long history of secularism and how it has shaped us, its disenchantment will continue flowing into our hearts and minds unnoticed.

A Brief History of Modern Unbelief

I am in no way saying that medieval Christians had it all together. Nor were they some shining example of theological perfection. Ironically, it was the well-meaning ideas of medieval Christian theologians that started our zigzag course to the secular age. One of those well-meaning ideas was a theological movement called "nominalism."

I regard the birth of nominalism as one of the great disasters of Western Christianity. To understand nominalism, however, it's best if we begin with how medieval Christians perceived things before nominalism appeared. Acclaimed scholar Thomas Howard writes this about the medieval Christian mind-set:

> This mind fancied that everything meant everything, and that it all rushed up finally to heaven. We have an idea of royalty, this mind said, which we observe in our politics and which we attribute to lions and eagles, and we have this idea because there is a great King at the top of things, and he has set things thus so that our fancies will be drawn toward his royal Person, and we will recognize the hard realities of which the stuff of our world has been a poor shadow when we stumble into his royal court.[7]

In other words, the medieval Christian mind took the Bible seriously when, in many places, from the Old Testament to the New Testament, it talked about the earth and its goodness being a faint copy of the ultimate reality of God's perfection in heaven. Yes, Greek philosophy touched on this concept too. Plato had stumbled on a part of the truth when he imagined a universal, eternal reality hiding behind the finite. But he was eating in the dark—only nibbling at the edges of a great feast without finding its center.

When the great scourge of nominalism came, led in part by the well-meaning voice of Christian theologian William of Ockham in the late 1200s and early 1300s, he planted the seeds for the medieval Christian mind to lose its enchantment. He taught a philosophy that, when combined with other teachings, removed the innate God-focused meaning in things. The natural world stopped being a point-marker to things beyond the physical world. As Robin Phillips, author of *Saints and Scoundrels*, writes:

Sadly, many Christians—Protestant evangelicals, Roman Catholics, and Eastern Orthodox alike—have imbibed various forms of nominalism, theological voluntarism and divine command theory which have oriented them to perceive the world as essentially a collection of disconnected particulars but with no intrinsic teleology integral to, and discoverable within, the created order. Instead, order is seen to be imposed extrinsically through mere fiat by the raw injunctions of God. But moral order that is imposed on creation is not order at all, but isolated commands that might just have easily been otherwise. According to this more nominalist understanding of the world (which again, is often more implicit than explicit), while creation may not be evil, it is without inherent meaning and therefore not fully "good" in the most complete sense.[8]

Of course, Ockham's concerns about the church's use of Greek philosophy were understandable too. Thomas Aquinas and his realism crowd, along with many other Christians of his day, were absorbing Greek philosophy and finding ways to synthesize it into the teaching of the Bible. Besides provoking misguided reactions, like Ockham's awful nominalism, the Christian scholars of that period were beginning to isolate philosophical knowledge as something separate from sacred knowledge—something that could be developed to the fullness of wisdom without any help from the Word and the Holy Spirit.

They were beginning to elevate human reason.

Along with all this, the Protestant Reformation came, and, in some ways, functioned as a black swan event—an unexpected explosion and rearrangement of the spiritual terrain.

All of these things opened the gates for an ambitious new project that none of these Christian scholars intended to kick-start: the methodical, centuries-long construction of a secular humanist civilization. The massive scaffolding of our secular age is one of the most impressive projects ever accomplished in human history. It's right up there with the Tower of Babel.

In fact, the construction of exclusive humanism, as Taylor proves in *A Secular Age*,[9] was not a subtraction story as many atheists claim today. Exclusive humanism was not the inevitable course of humanity that finally happened after we removed our silly religious superstitions. That's the subtraction myth.

History shows us that it was an addition story—a hugely

ambitious project led by a lineage of determined individuals who navigated a long, zigzagging path of history. Once Christian theologians mistakenly abandoned important theological ground and moved away from a sacramental mind-set, the wolves began to stream in. Most of these wolves were apostates (former Christians who left the faith and actively opposed it)—men who zealously yearned to push the world away from a God-centered order.

In the book *Apostate: The Men Who Destroyed the Christian West*, author Kevin Swanson provides a chronological list of some of these men. It reads like a genealogy—a rough sketch of exclusive humanism's family tree. It tells a spellbinding tale of how humanity patiently built its new Tower of Babel, the great structure of secular humanism that stands today, one stone at a time.

Every major figure involved in the project had one common thread: they all elevated the authority of human reason above God. Although it's beyond the scope of this book to unpack in detail what Swanson writes about each man, the chronological list in his table of contents[10] is telling:

- René Descartes (1596–1650), philosophy
- John Locke (1632–1704), theology
- Jean-Jacques Rousseau (1712–1778), society planning
- Jeremy Bentham (1748–1832), John Stuart Mills (1806–1873, a disciple of Bentham), and Bertrand Russell (1872–1970, the godson of Mills), ethics and modern philosophy
- Ralph Waldo Emerson (1803–1882), the spiritual formation of the person
- Karl Marx (1818–1883), political theory

- Friedrich Nietzsche (1844–1900), psychology
- Charles Darwin (1809–1882), origin science
- John Dewey (1859–1952), education
- Jean-Paul Sartre (1905–1980), modern philosophy and culture

Swanson's list excludes some crucial names (for example, Sigmund Freud) because his focus was on apostates—former Christians. But even just the short list above illustrates Charles Taylor's point that the creation of the secular age is an addition story, not a subtraction story. The rise of exclusive humanism was an ambitious project that took generations to mature. The war against that sacramental mind-set—the transcendent longing of Joy that lies at the heart of this book—is not a new thing, in other words.

It has been going on for centuries.

Fighting Back that Hideous Strength

C. S. Lewis is still regarded today as one of the greatest scholars of medieval and Renaissance literature. He knew very well about the problem described above—about the treasures from the Middle Ages that were lost. He was particularly troubled by the rise of scientism. His book *That Hideous Strength*, Book Three in his beloved Space Trilogy, shows how scientism can indeed become diabolical and shift into one of the more sinister fruits of exclusive humanism.

In the story, a Cambridge don named Ransom Elwin, the man who was taken on adventures to Mars and Venus in the previous books, finds himself in a cosmic war on earth—though a much more subtle, invisible battle compared to his previous conflicts. His main opponent is an institute called N.I.C.E. (National Institute of Co-ordinated Experiments), which embodies a highly deceptive expression of scientism at its most lethal stage of maturity. During one particularly turbulent point in the story, we find Ransom pondering the conflict:

> It was this that kept the Director wakeful....Despair of objective truth had been increasingly insinuated into the scientists; indifference to it, and a concentration upon mere power, had been the result....Dreams of the far future destiny of man were dragging up from its shallow and unquiet grave the old dream of Man as God....What should they find incredible, since they believed no longer in a rational universe? What should they regard as too obscene, since they held that all morality was a mere subjective by-product of the physical and economic situations of men? The time was ripe. From the point of view which is accepted in Hell, the whole history of our Earth had led up to this moment.[11]

Lewis' depiction of the hubris of scientism or its diabolical intentions is not an exaggeration. In an essay by Martin Ryder in the *Encyclopedia of Science, Technology, and Ethics*, Ryder pinpoints the dangers of scientism when it's carried to its most ruthless logical conclusion:

> A scientistic culture privileges scientific knowledge over all other ways of knowing. It uses jargon, technical

language, and technical evidence in public debate as a means to exclude the laity from participation in policy formation. Despite such obvious transgressions of democracy, common citizens yield to the dictates of scientism without a fight. The norms of science abound in popular culture, and the naturalized authority of scientific reasoning can lead, if left unchecked, to a malignancy of cultural norms. The most notorious example of this was seen in Nazi Germany, where a noxious combination of scientism and utopianism led to the eugenics excesses of the Third Reich (Arendt 1951).[12]

The worship of human reason over God leads to self-refutation and eventually self-destruction, usually from the inevitable fall that comes after pride. In *That Hideous Strength*, Ransom observes how the wicked forces of N.I.C.E. have inadvertently opened the door to their own defeat because of their arrogance: "The Hideous Strength holds all this Earth in its fist to squeeze as it wishes. But for their one mistake, there would be no hope left. If of their own evil will they had not broken the frontier and let in the celestial Powers, this would be their moment of victory. Their own strength has betrayed them. They have gone to the gods who would not have come to them, and pulled down Deep Heaven on their heads."[13]

In the midst of these dangers—in the midst of the tremendous cross-pressures of the secular age—our journey through grief and Joy can easily become disenchanted. We should not underestimate the force of these cross-pressures. However, at the same time, we should not discount God's ability to change the situation and re-enchant our lives, and our culture, with his wonder and glory.

The solution is not a series of self-help programs. Our hope is not in a top-down transformation of our culture through politics. It is a grassroots movement that rises from deep aquifers of the Holy Spirit. It is a posture of the heart. It is humility. It is brokenness.

It is prayer.

The Contrary Motion of a Praying Heart

In the U2 song "If God Will Send His Angels," we find a powerful metaphor for prayer—and our need for this solution. The song appears on *Pop*, the 1997 follow-up to their album *Zooropa*. *Pop* was the final album in U2's electronic trash-pop trilogy that began with *Achtung Baby*. "If God Will Send His Angels" is one of the best songs from the album, and part of its success comes from something called "contrary motion." Its skillful use of contrary motion acts out the meaning of the song's lyrics, which present a tearful, psalm-like plea of prayer before God.

When two melodies—a high melody and a low melody—move closer to each other, the top one sinking down and the bottom one rising up, it is called contrary motion. This contrary motion, in the lyrical context of this song, reminds us how badly we need to fall on our knees in prayer and rely on God instead of standing on our feet and relying on ourselves. This skyward reliance is expressed most clearly in the discipline of intercessory prayer, in which a person prays persistently and passionately about a problem.

In fact, Jesus devoted an entire parable to the principle "that men always ought to pray and not lose heart" (Luke 18:1–8). As pain and darkness overwhelm us, we shouldn't reach for our coping mechanisms. We shouldn't numb the feelings by plugging our heads into ZooTV. We shouldn't rely on the wisdom of humanity to make everything better again. Instead, we should fall to our knees and bring our brokenness to God day and night without giving up. We should take the advice of 1 Peter 5:6–7: "Humble yourselves under the mighty hand of God, that He may exalt you in due time, casting all your care upon Him, for He cares for you."

Our knees and heart go down.

Our prayers go up.

Contrary motion.

The song "If God Will Send His Angels" acts this out for us with its vocal and guitar melodies. It becomes an outward symbol of a spiritual reality. The shape of Bono's vocal line moves down. But the melodic shape of The Edge's guitar moves up. They repeat this contrary motion through every verse and chorus—a relentless, persistent melodic shape.

Whenever Bono's low-gliding voice drifts down, we hear The Edge pop the lead guitar line into the high register. The contrast catches our attention and adds a subtle drama to the music. And their contrary motion matches the lyrical theme of the song: Bono is sinking to his knees while lifting up a prayer, pouring his heart out to God like the psalmist. He's surveying the emptiness and corruption of the age, and perhaps in himself, and crying out to God to send a sign of hope—a sign that God has a plan to use all things for good despite all the suffering and wickedness (Rom. 8:26–28).

The song expresses a deep pain over the disenchantment and immanence of our secular age and the shallowness of commercialized religion—an exhausted, cynical acknowledgment of just how difficult it can be to apprehend the joy of Christ in the modern world.

If we cry out to God with the desperate childlike cry of U2's "If God Will Send His Angels," if we embrace the contrary motion of prayer, and if we pray without giving up, then he will come and fill our hearts with wonder again. We'll see how the world, and the people around us, are charged with his grandeur. This in turn will preserve the Joy that God has been building in our lives. The Joy will become an even brighter point-marker to the reality beyond this world.

What Hans Boersma said about the medieval Christians will then become true of us. We will become convinced that the universe, and our existence in it, finds its reality and identity in Christ and not in human reason. This will open our eyes to see God's truth, goodness, and beauty in the world around us.[14]

We will have a sacramental mind-set.

Once we have that kind of vision, the Holy Spirit can take us safely to the next Stage of Joy: the Longing for Truth.

The Stages of Joy Playlist

7. "If God Will Send His Angels" from the album *Pop*. Summary: The secular age has disenchanted us and severed God's

grandeur from the world. The contrary motion of prayer reconnects what has been severed and preserves Joy.

Scripture

"In the beginning was the Word, and the Word was with God, and the Word was God. He was with God in the beginning. Through him all things were made; without him nothing was made that has been made" (John 1:1–3 NIV).

Notes for the Quest

In this passage, the apostle John tells us the meaning of life, and the meaning of life is Christ. Through him, the Author of Life, everything was made. The wise sages of the world rejected this claim in Jesus' day, just as they reject it now. The modern age might seem open-minded, but it has one very stringent rule: no one is allowed to know the meaning of life—or at least claim to know it. Certainty is no longer accepted. Any declarations of absolute truth have become forbidden in the hubs of culture.

It takes courage to stand against that cultural riptide, but it is worth it. When we see the world charged with the grandeur of God and when we wade into the depths of meaning that Christ has hidden in the universe, life carries a constant richness. Gratitude comes easy, as does a healthy brokenness. We don't ignore the pain around us. The spiritual darkness of the world breaks our hearts, and we learn that the safest, most secure place for us is on our knees in prayer, crying out to God.

A Prayer for the Journey

Abba Father, open my eyes to see your grandeur, not only in the universe but also in my life. Show me all the little wonders you've done over the years—the things you've done that I never noticed or was too hard-hearted to sense. Reveal the Easter eggs of meaning that you've hidden all around me, even in the painful circumstances. Help me to see that you are able to use all things for good and infuse all things with new meaning, even my deepest sorrows. In Jesus' name, amen.

More Bible Verses for the Road

Romans 1:20; Luke 18:1–8; 1 Peter 5:6–7; Romans 8:26–28

CHAPTER 9

ALONG A BEAM
OF ULTRAVIOLET LIGHT

*Such is the tragi-comedy of our situation—we continue
to clamour for those very qualities we are rendering
impossible....In a sort of ghastly simplicity we remove the
organ and demand the function. We make men without
chests and expect of them virtue and enterprise. We laugh
at honour and are shocked to find traitors in our midst.
We castrate and bid the geldings be fruitful.*
– C. S. Lewis, The Abolition of Man

Song to cue: "Ultraviolet (Light My Way)"
from the album *Achtung Baby*

B efore I can go any further, I must confess something.
I have become thoroughly weary of the Internet. There
are still days when I love it, sure—especially the ability to
video stream with family—but a creeping sense of horror has
tainted the whole thing.

I am especially weary of the trolling I occasionally encounter as a writer for media outlets: the knee-jerk comments, the
acrimonious criticism, the fly-by-night assessments born from a

kiddie pool depth of research and forethought, and the way the anonymity of the Internet makes people vicious. I am weary of our rampant mobile device addiction. And I am certainly not blameless in these things. At times I have been guilty of knee-jerk, emotional responses online. Most of us have at one time or another. Yes, a spiritual ZooTV distracts us. Tragically, the secular age disenchants us.

But something else is happening.

The world is short-circuiting our ability to make sound judgments and to search for the truth with patience, depth of thinking, and wisdom. Slowly, post by post, tweet by tweet, raging comment by raging comment, the screen age is training us to live an easily manipulated existence controlled by a million emotional triggers.

It's terrifying.

It's also bringing out the beasts that we've been hiding in dungeons beneath our smiles. Some of the nicest people we know in person suddenly transform into vicious, merciless trolls online.

But the problem goes beyond the Internet. The digital world is merely an amplifier for a habit that's always been with us. Deep within our nature, a fissure of self-centeredness boils. It's what drives us to project our own needs onto others instead of seeing their true condition. It's those self-absorbed habits we nurture in conversation—such as when someone is talking, and instead of listening closely, we are thinking about what our next reply will be.

We give cursory attention to others. All the while our eyes are turned inward, always staring at ourselves. We become so fixated with Self that our assessments of other people become shallow, inaccurate, and full of presumptions. This impatient self-absorption also pushes us to make rash judgments about situations in our lives—or even about God himself.

C. S. Lewis addressed this problem directly. In his essay "Meditation in a Toolshed," published in the book *God in the Dock: Essays on Theology and Ethics*, Lewis recounts a moment spent in a toolshed earlier in the day before sitting down to write. As he stood inside the nearly pitch-black shed, a beam of sunlight passed through a crack at the top of the door. It was the only thing visible—just a long beam with specks of dust floating in it.

The longer he stood outside of the beam staring at it, the darker the shed seemed to be. The beam was not helping him see because he was not looking along the ray of light. He was "seeing the beam, not seeing things by it." He writes: "Then I moved, so that the beam fell on my eyes. Instantly the whole previous picture vanished. I saw no toolshed, and (above all) no beam. Instead I saw, framed in the irregular cranny at the top of the door, green leaves moving on the branches of a tree outside and beyond that, 90 odd million miles away, the sun. Looking along the beam, and looking at the beam are very different experiences."[1]

This sums up our modern way of assessing the people, things, and situations around us. We look at them. We do not look alongside them. We resist the hard work of imaginative empathy—that laborious art form of becoming so self-forgetful and so intensely others-minded that not only do we step into their shoes, but we also immerse ourselves in their vantage point completely. We're not giving a blanket endorsement of their beliefs or lifestyles, but we're baptizing our imaginations in their experience. We're committing ourselves to understand what it feels like to be them—just as committed as God was when he entered into our sufferings by becoming one of us and experiencing the world as we do.

Not only do we blur our view of others when we look at the beam and not along it, but we also blur our view of truth.

In his toolshed essay, Lewis uses the example of the religion versus atheism debate. He notes how the modern mind tends to look at the beam of faith and draw self-assured conclusions about religion without looking along the beam of faith. In fact, those who look along the beam are often ridiculed:

> The people who look at things have had it all their own way; the people who look along things have simply been brow-beaten....."All these moral ideals which look so transcendental and beautiful from inside," says the wiseacre, "are really only a mass of biological instincts and inherited taboos." And no one plays the game the other way round by replying, "If you will only step inside, the things that look to you like instincts and taboos will suddenly reveal their real and transcendental nature." That, in fact, is the whole basis of the specifically "modern" type of thought.[2]

There is a strange mode of detachment in the secular age. We make judgments about people, places, things, and beliefs without ever stepping inside them as much as our imaginations will allow. As a part-time movie critic, too often I see people going online and trashing a film before they've seen it. Or if they've seen the film, they spend very little time looking along the beam that the film was creating. I've felt the seducing pull to do this in my own reviews.

Lewis, in his book *An Experiment in Criticism*, used the way we look at paintings as an example of this problem: "We sit down before the picture in order to have something done to us, not that we may do things with it. The first demand any work of any art makes upon us is surrender. Look. Listen. Receive. Get yourself out of the way. (There is no good asking first whether the work before you deserves such a surrender, for until you have surrendered you cannot possibly find out.)"[3]

In a similar way, the Holy Spirit has a specific purpose for the Stages of Joy, but we must be willing to receive it. This is where the next stage, the Longing for Truth, comes to help us.

The Longing for Truth

The Longing for Truth begins with humility and surrender. It begins with small steps: you choose to listen earnestly to someone online or in person instead of arguing with them, for example. This is a promising sign, an indication that the Longing for Truth is pulling on your heart. You feel a desire to look along the beam. You're tired of always looking at things. You want to step inside them.

This humble Longing, if you continue to follow where it leads, will take you to something grand. It will grow to massive proportions. You will suddenly want to look along the beam of creation itself—to see the grand tapestry of meaning that encloses you on every side, and to see how everything in the caused world, from the galaxies beyond the Milky Way to the sea stars in the tide pool, work as point-markers to the Uncaused Someone behind it. It's a gnawing hunger for transcendent truth, and it is deeply dissatisfied with the secular age's shallow fixation on immanence.

The sacramental mind-set mentioned in chapter 8 clears the path for this Longing for Truth to flourish. This mind-set pushes away the now-is-all-that-matters thinking and calmly sets aside the God-is-dead claim, and then insists boldly that the world is indeed charged with God's grandeur. It insists that the primary purpose of the world is to get our attention on heaven—on transcendence, not immanence.

The universe is a giant arrow pointing away from itself. It's an exit sign on a freeway pointing us to our true home. And that home is certainly not the freeway. We must look elsewhere. We must look beyond creation. We must look to heaven as if our lives depend on it. As Hans Boersma writes:

> In contemporary Western theology, however, discourse on "heaven" has lost its central place. Evangelicals and Catholics alike have become more focused on the here-and-now than on the then-and-there. To speak of creaturely participation in heavenly realities ("heavenly participation") cannot but come across as outlandish to an age whose horizons have narrowed to such an extent that bodily goods, cultural endeavors, and political achievements have become matters of ultimate concern.[4]

The Longing for Truth, therefore, and its sacramental mind-set, leads to a way of life wholly different from anything this world can offer. Yes, we are quick to listen and slow to speak, as James 1:16–20 exhorts, but becoming good listeners is just the beginning. We instinctively yearn to look along the beam of not only every person but also every *thing* around us. We see how the natural world is just one big beam of sunlight passing through a crack in the toolshed door.

If we resolve to step into the beam and look along it instead of only looking at it, we will find that everything reveals him. Each marvel in creation—from the wild oddity and power of subatomic physics to the wiggle and waddle of a sea otter—carries a beacon that points to some hidden beauty in Yahweh, and we strive to search it out.

The more we discover the little cosmic love notes hidden like Easter eggs throughout the world, the more we experience the sharp pangs of Joy. As a side effect, we become more curious about life and the world around us. We become quick to listen to what creation is saying about its Creator. And it is saying plenty. Just one small branch of the physical world—sound waves—has taught me volumes of spiritual lessons about Christ. And this shouldn't surprise me, especially when I read this about God: "All things were made through Him, and without Him nothing was made that was made" (John 1:3).

This new cosmic inquisitiveness, this Longing for Truth that expects to find point-markers to God in everything around us, will also change the way we experience suffering. It stirs something similar to the appetite of a treasure hunter.

Each day, instead of obsessing over bleak negativity, we look with eagerness to discover flickers of the Author of Life in everything—to see traces of his activity in our lives in every detail of our routine, whether we're going to a doctor's appointment, seeing a movie with friends, or stargazing. In other words, we don't let this Longing for Truth float by us passively and then vanish. We capture it and stoke the flame the moment we sense the heat.

And then something curious happens. The more we look along the beam of heaven, the more the beam bends outward. Our eyes, by some miracle, are beginning to move off ourselves.

We're becoming less selfish.

Looking Along the Beam of Others

In the beginning of our quest through the Stages of Joy—as we heard the call of "Where The Streets Have No Name"—a longing moved us toward something vague and nameless. Its glow at the end of the horizon pulled us forward. It threw a wild longing into our rib cages. This yearning ignited an inconsolable motion, and we set off running, though we knew not where.

But now the destination is beginning to take shape—partly, at least. The inconsolable motion is becoming more about others. It is sending us out. The Longing for Truth becomes a Longing for the Truth-of-Others—a hunger to know the hurts of others. We discover people who are bleeding from the same wounds that we've sustained. The Spirit gives us timely words and ways to encourage them, to help them go further in their journey through the Stages of Joy—or help them take their first steps.

Ultimately, this Longing for the Truth-of-Others makes us look along the beam. We've stopped the habit of always looking at people. Our empathy has been jolted awake with new powers of imagination, and we're seeing the world through the eyes of other people with stunning detail.

This sets off new fires of inconsolable motion in our hearts. We're moved to go out and do whatever we can to help those who have stirred our empathy. And then as our journey through Joy becomes a mission, it changes the value of our suffering. It repurposes it and transforms it into something precious: a life raft for shipwrecked souls.

Ultraviolet (and Other Sonic Tone Colors)

The U2 song "Ultraviolet (Light My Way)" teaches us something vivid and powerful about looking along the beam. The song has always been my favorite track from the 1990s masterpiece *Achtung Baby* (it's tied with "So Cruel" and "Trying To Throw Your Arms Around The World").

The Edge's guitar recaptures his galloping echo sound of the 1980s. It shimmers, bounces, splits, and multiplies into a surging headwater of music that spills over everything it meets. Or perhaps it's more like the chain reaction of a detonation. The notes reproduce exponentially, like atoms bouncing off each other until they reach critical mass. It's the same echoing inconsolable motion found in "Where The Streets Have No Name."

But there's something different about "Ultraviolet (Light My Way)." It has a different tone color—an electrified neon glow. In past incarnations of the classic U2 guitar sound, we heard a more straight-forward affair: just a clean electric, echoing guitar part spilling over the stereo field, backed by basic drums and bass, and an earnest Bono marching through his high tenor range. But in this song, Bono drifts down into the low, seedy side of town, quietly musing through his lyrics and ruminating in the bottom half of his range.

His voice sounds like a lonely man wandering the streets of East Berlin at night in the winter, thinking over the ruins of his life while recalling the lost love of a woman who had, for so long, lit his way through the darkness. When you're used to hearing the usual shouting Bono accompany The Edge, this strange combination of low-drifting Bono and high-sprinting guitar catches you off guard.

But there's more.

A low synth part adds yet another color to the mix. As its brooding hum moves beneath the guitar's stream of high notes, the synth feels attached to the slow-drifting vocals. It's stealthy and subdued, and at the end of every measure it moves through a few notes—a little turn of a motif like the curl of an eyelash or the twirl of a quarter through a magician's fingers—and it paints over the classic U2 sound with an electric blue, ultraviolet color. One part melancholy, one part hopeful.

The combination of all the colors—the classic high echo of the guitar, the drifting vocals, the bluish neon brood of synth notes—blends into a new color that neither instrument could have created on its own. When all the parts add up, the song creates its own shade of ultraviolet—one of the most interesting tone colors that U2 has splashed onto the canvas.

For something like this to happen, of course, each musician must be willing to surrender some of his color presence in the mix to make room for new instruments. As each instrument yields to another instrument, the color morphs into something new.

U2 has long made a career out of this technique of tone color and sonic texture, but they certainly weren't the first. In fact, one of the most notable composers of modern orchestral music, Japanese composer Toru Takemitsu, was known as a master of "painting" works of musical art using carefully blended tone color.

He made tone colors and slow-shifting hues of sound the centerpiece of his compositions rather than the traditional forms of harmony and melody. He recognized how an instrument—a trombone, for example—might have a yellow tone in the mind's eye, but another instrument, such as the middle to high range of a French horn, might have a light blue tone color. However, when he has these two instruments play the same notes together, the yellow and blue tones mix and a new greenish sound appears in the mind. The instruments surrender to one another and allow a temporary destruction of each other's color so that a new tone color can be created.

When We Glow with the Grandeur of God

This approach of tone color composition becomes a metaphor. It demonstrates the power of yielding to a union that produces something new. It is a generalized metaphor, yes—and many people could make use of it in different ways—but it helps us see C. S. Lewis' specific point from a fresh angle.

Imaginative empathy can be a beautiful, powerful doorway to understanding others and communicating effectively. This is not about surrendering our convictions. It is about learning to see and experience the convictions of others as they see and experience them—to obey the biblical command to be quick to listen and slow to speak. We must not resist the push of Joy that sends us outside of ourselves into the lives of others, as messy as it all might be.

We desperately need this, not just for ourselves but also for the sake of our culture. Disenchantment has fallen over Western civilization, and the grandeur of God has been severed from the modern mind. The appearance of a meaningless world without God adds an icy sting to the experience of grief.

An excruciating pain throbs in our culture's chest, and the culture does whatever it can to numb it. However, the Great Physician knows the right medicine, and the Stages of Joy are a part of it. Joy will awaken a Longing for Truth and a Longing for the Truth-of-Others—to the sorrows of those around you.

As my dad, Don Ott, once wrote in a letter about ministry, "I pray that the Lord would love his people through you." As God uses you to help others, don't be shocked when you discover that he has charged you with his grandeur just as he has charged creation. Suddenly you become a sign or symbol of a glorious spiritual reality—a sacramental lighthouse, an ambassador of his glory to a world desperate for the smallest glimpse of it.

The Stages of Joy Playlist

8. "Ultraviolet (Light My Way)" from the album *Achtung Baby*. Summary: Joy leads to a Longing for Truth and for the Truth-of-Others—the hunger and ability to see God's grandeur in the things and people around us.

Scripture

"Therefore, since we have a great high priest who has ascended into heaven, Jesus the Son of God, let us hold firmly to the faith we profess. For we do not have a high priest who is unable to empathize with our weaknesses, but we have one who has been tempted in every way, just as we are—yet he did not sin. Let us then approach God's throne of grace with confidence, so that we may receive mercy and find grace to help us in our time of need" (Heb. 4:14–16 NIV).

Notes for the Quest

God became a man not only to die for us but also to experience all of the heartache and grubby discomfort of this world. God baptized himself in nerve endings. He threw himself into our sundering sea. In fact, Christ's baptism in the River Jordan was a baptism of identification.

As John the Baptist so well knew, Christ had no need of baptism or repentance. The Son of God did it to show us one of the reasons why he had come into the world: to be immersed in the human experience and to empathize with us. If God went to that much trouble to know our sufferings and empathize with our weaknesses—to truly see what our perspective looks like—how much more should we strive to enter the experiences and convictions of others with empathy and vivid imagination?

A Prayer for the Journey

Abba Father, please break my habit of looking at things instead of looking along them. Fill my spirit with an insatiable hunger to look along the beam of creation until I see you in everything around me and in every circumstance, even the painful ones. When I am with others, please slow the knee-jerk responses within me, and give me the patient empathy that Jesus displayed in his ministry. Stir my imagination and soften my heart to step into the perspectives of others instead of making rash, clumsy judgments. In Jesus' name, amen.

More Bible Verses for the Road

James 1:19–21

Kevin and his wife, Amy, took the following pictures at U2's concert at the Rose Bowl in Pasadena, California, during the band's 360° Tour on October 25, 2009:

PART IV

Every Breaking Wave:
When the
Flesh Is Weak

WHERE WE ARE ON THE MAP:
A SUMMARY OF PART III

- Our digital age threatens to numb our hearts, stop our journey through Joy, and poison how we grieve. To overcome it, we must allow Christ's rule to create boundaries in our lives.

- The secular age has disenchanted us and severed God's grandeur from the world. The contrary motion of prayer reconnects what has been severed and preserves Joy.

- Joy leads to a Longing for Truth and for the Truth-of-Others—the hunger and ability to see God's grandeur in the things and people around us.

CHAPTER 10

OVERWHELMED, OUT OF CONTROL, AND A NEW YEAR'S DAY IN THE PEWS

Songs to cue: "Out Of Control"
from the album *Boy*

"New Year's Day"
from the album *War*

C. S. Lewis was a powerful ambassador of God's glory to the world, and God used him to do extraordinary things. However, when we see someone like Lewis, it becomes easy to discount ourselves. Amid the widespread praise of Lewis' genius, we must not make him a god. We cannot fall for the idea that God was only able to use Lewis—and therefore cannot use us—because he was utterly brilliant and seemed to have all of his moral ducks in a row every day of his life.

The reality is that Lewis was only human—and every human soul has its limits. He faced situations that were too much to handle, that overwhelmed and crushed him. I don't buy the slogan "God never gives us more than we can handle." The opposite is true, in fact; he almost always gives us more than we can handle. How else can he melt away our self-reliance and teach us to rely on him?

For example, in Lewis' case, the death of his new wife, Helen Joy Davidman, just after they had floated away on Cupid's weightlessness—after only a few years of newlywed abundance and the gliding new gleam of togetherness—was certainly more than Lewis could handle. Madeleine L'Engle, in her forward for *A Grief Observed*, said it this way:

> When C. S. Lewis married Joy Davidman, she was in the hospital. He knew that he was marrying a woman who was dying of cancer. And even though there was the unexpected remission, and some good years of reprieve, his experience of marriage was only a taste....He had been invited to the great feast of marriage and the banquet was rudely snatched away from him before he had done more than sample the hors d'oeuvres.[1]

The blow of his wife's death caused a momentary loss of faith. It knocked his entire mental and emotional apparatus ajar, and, astonishingly, he recorded the details of the event in journal form—writings that would be published under a pen name N. W. Clerk in the book *A Grief Observed*.

We witness something perhaps a bit horrifying in this little diary: we see the heart and mind of C. S. Lewis bend and buckle under the weight of his rage and sorrow. At times it's almost too much to bear, especially for a reader who has loved his books. He doesn't seem himself. His writing voice is not the same. There is a spat of vengeful ill will toward God in some parts—a raging sea hiding beneath his tone. Contrast, for example, one passage from *The Problem of Pain*, published in 1940, with passages from *A Grief Observed*, published in 1961. From *The Problem of Pain*:

> Now God, who has made us, knows what we are and that our happiness lies in Him. Yet we will not seek it in Him as long as He leaves us any other resort where it can even plausibly be looked for. While what we call "our own life" remains agreeable we will not surrender it to Him. What then can God do in our interests but make "our own life" less agreeable to us, and take away the plausible source of false happiness? It is just here, where God's providence seems at first to be most cruel, that the Divine humility, the stooping down of the Highest, most deserves praise.[2]

From *A Grief Observed*:

> Why do I make room in my mind for such filth and nonsense? Do I hope that if feeling disguises itself as thought I shall feel less? Aren't all these notes the senseless writhings of a man who won't accept the fact that there is nothing we can do with suffering except to suffer it? Who still thinks there is some device (if only he could find it) which will make pain not to be pain. It doesn't really matter whether you grip the arms of the dentist's chair or let your hands lie in your lap. The drill drills on.[3]

And then this second passage from *A Grief Observed*:

> If my house has collapsed at one blow, that is because it was a house of cards. The faith which "took these things into account" was not faith but imagination. The taking them into account was not real sympathy. If I had really cared, as I thought I did, about the sorrows of the world, I should not have been so overwhelmed when my own sorrow came. It has been an imaginary faith playing with innocuous counters labelled "Illness," "Pain," "Death," and "Loneliness."[4]

Lewis eventually did pull through and reclaim a strong belief in all that he had written about in *The Problem of Pain*, and how he pulled through will be explored in the final chapters of this book. But when we see such vulnerability and normal questioning in such a giant of the faith, it's encouraging, even awe-inspiring, to remember that God used this fallen human being—a mortal with cracks in the armor just like the rest of us—to speak tremendous life to the entire population of the United Kingdom in her darkest hour.

In other words, if God can use C. S. Lewis to accomplish great things, he can use us too—even if we have a "house of cards" hiding somewhere in our weak hearts as Lewis did.

Not Just Churchill:
When God Raises Up a Voice for a Nation

Prime Minister Winston Churchill was not the only one speaking strength and courage to a desperate people during World War II. In the stormy period between 1942 and 1944, C. S.

Lewis was an unexpected blast of sunlight. In the midst of the horrors of war, a booming, oaky British accent tinged with the curled tone of Belfast filled the airwaves across the United Kingdom as Lewis began speaking to the nation through regular broadcasts on the BBC.[5]

His sturdy voice and clarion beams of thought caught the attention of the world as he spoke life and truth about Jesus, reality, heaven, ethics, and the claims of Christianity as they actually are, not as the modern world often depicts them. In 1947, he appeared on the cover of *Time* magazine,[6] and his wartime BBC broadcasts were later adapted into the classic book *Mere Christianity*. Lewis was a godsend for a nation—even a world—in need.

During times of upheaval, God knows that we can't do it on our own. We need encouragement, and he sends voices. He sends prophets not only to nations but also to his weary sheep—voices impregnated with his voice. The precious sound of it pulls us out of the madness, back onto solid footing.

We need these lifelines more than we care to admit. No matter how hard we try, times of great sorrow will inevitably wear on us. We get weak. We lose the horizon. An inner nausea, a spiritual sickness, takes hold. And no matter how well we move along in the quest outlined in this book, our most formidable enemy, ourselves, always puts up a brutal fight. Inevitably, days come when no amount of anything—deep-hearted longing, joy, prayer, study, or service to others—can hold back the rockslide.

We collapse.

Emotional exhaustion sets in. Chronic anxiety, stress, or irrational fear follow. We feel like we're falling apart. Nothing helps. (Even then, God never leaves us. As my mom put it so well, "Thank goodness he still loves me, even in my usual crumpled state!")[7]

This is when the Longing for Truth aids us—a Longing that can cut through these moments of collapse at the speed of thought. It reminds us that our faith is built on the Solid Rock of the Word, not on our feelings. It reminds us that God's truth is never too far out of reach. We see a wonderful promise in Jesus' teachings: "Blessed are those who hunger and thirst for righteousness, for they will be filled" (Matt. 5:6 NIV).

The reason is simple: absolute truth finds its root not in an abstract idea but in a Person—in God. The Holy Spirit, our Wonderful Counselor, knows how to relate the truth to us when we need it the most—whether through a verse that he brings to our attention, a book, a song, a painting, a timely word from someone we know, or an unexpected encouragement from a complete stranger. The Truth of truths, the Word of words, is not a stale, lifeless idea from the mind of Plato hidden away on the top shelf of a library.

The Truth of truths and the Word of words once became skin and blood and bones and overcame death. He is living and active, and the Spirit's ability to adapt to our needs at any given moment far exceeds—and always will exceed—any artificial intelligence or smart app. Even in the confusing maelstrom of grief and sorrow that jostles us around, the active movement of the Word draws nearer to us. It is reaching for us moment by moment.

With this wonderful reality in mind, when we survey the many tools that the Holy Spirit has used in human history, Lewis' masterpiece *Mere Christianity*—the book that came from his BBC talks—is a work of artisan craft. The book simplifies intricate, complex truths into life rafts with large handles that are easy to grasp even when you're rushing downstream in the chaos and reaching out to grab onto something in desperation.

For example, in chapter 7 of *Mere Christianity*, Lewis reveals something practical that we can do in the situations described above, when our weaknesses, character flaws, and the world have worn us down and overwhelmed us.

We can pretend to be like Christ.

We can put him on (Rom. 13:14), like a child at play with costumes, until the pretending becomes reality.

Lewis begins this whole line of thought with a fairy tale about a person with an ugly face who wears a mask. After wearing the mask for years, the ugly man finds that his face has grown to fit the mask, and his appearance has changed. He has become handsome. As Lewis writes, "What had begun as disguise had become a reality."[8] Lewis ties this idea to the act of praying the Lord's Prayer, which begins by boldly addressing God as "Our Father":

> Its very first words are Our Father. Do you now see what those words mean? They mean quite frankly, that you are putting yourself in the place of a son of God. To put it bluntly, you are dressing up as Christ. If you like, you are pretending. Because, of course, the moment you realise what the words mean, you realise that you are not a son of God…you are a bundle of self-centered fears, hopes, greeds, jealousies, and self-conceit, all doomed to death. So that, in a way, this dressing up as Christ is a piece

of outrageous cheek. But the odd thing is that He has ordered us to do it.[9]

Of course, there are two kinds of pretending, Lewis reminds us. There is the dishonest pretending, when we lie to a friend and say we will help them move out of their house on Tuesday, but we have no intention of doing so. But there is also a wonderfully fruitful kind of pretending—an earnest, determined kind that wants the pretending to be true. Lewis explains the good kind this way:

When you are not feeling particularly friendly but know you ought to be, the best thing you can do, very often, is to put on a friendly manner and behave as if you were a nicer person than you actually are. And in a few minutes, as we have all noticed, you will be really feeling friendlier than you were. Very often the only way to get a quality in reality is to start behaving as if you had it already. That is why children's games are so important. They are always pretending to be grown-ups—playing soldiers, playing shop. But all the time, they are hardening their muscles and sharpening their wits so that the pretence of being grown-up helps them to grow up in earnest.[10]

This is the answer that comes to our aid when our emotional and mental states have failed us. Our momentary inner reality—whether or not there is an agreeable thought or emotion inside of us—no longer becomes our hope. Our internal state is no longer the fount of reality. Christ is our hope. And he turns defeats into triumphs.

When I interviewed Christian recording artist Plumb about how God miraculously restored her marriage after she and her husband separated, she said this about what happens when everything in life breaks down: "I just wrote a song…it's called 'Broken Places,' and it says, 'you're strong in the broken places.' That's where he does his best. And so whatever is broken in you or broken in your life, just think about that—that God can actually be strong in that completely fractured or shattered place."[11]

As long as God exists, as long as he is living and active, and as long as there is some action, big or small, that we can choose that imitates his nature (whether we feel like doing it or not), there is hope. It is no longer about working down a to-do list until we feel a strong sense of self-satisfaction about our righteousness. It's not about mustering up the right kind of feelings inside to match our external declarations.

It's about imitating a Person, like a child admiringly imitates an adult. It is about simply watching him and pretending to be a son of God just as he is. Children do this every day in their games. Artists do it with their work when they try to capture someone's image in a portrait. As Lewis writes, "You are no longer thinking simply about right and wrong; you are trying to catch the good infection from a Person. It is more like painting a portrait than like obeying a set of rules."[12]

Out of Control

Speaking of children, when U2's band members were just boys in the 1970s working on an album called, coincidentally, *Boy*, they wrote the song "Out Of Control." This song captures in sketch form the jarring, off-kilter reality of life. You can hear the youthful energy plunging forward recklessly off-balance and wild. If Bono didn't sing a single word about the wildness of life and growing up or being out of control, you would still grasp all of those concepts in the music alone.

In music theory jargon, the song accomplishes this effect using wild interval leaps in its melody and rhythmic syncopation. The melody jumps all over the place with leaps and spasms, springing from a low note to a high note without warning, and then hopping back down, and then up again—and while Bono does this with all the gleeful abandon of a teenager set free for the weekend, the rhythm of the drums, bass, and guitar stomps forward with determination as if it were trying to walk on a ship in a violent storm.

The stormy youth that U2 was writing about was not, however, the typical teenage angst. It found its turbulence in the violence of Dublin, Ireland, when people were setting off bombs and killing other people not far from where Bono lived. U2's 2014 album *Songs Of Innocence* spends much of its time looking back on that jarring, off-kilter, out-of-control experience of growing up in Dublin.

As Bono writes in the *Songs Of Innocence* liner notes, "Ireland in the '70s was a tough place. On any other Friday at 5:30pm in 1974 I would have been on Talbot Street in a record shop. On May 17th I rode my bike to school that day and dodged one of the bloodiest moments in a history that divided an island…3 car bombs coordinated to detonate at the same time destroyed Dublin's city centre."[13]

A 1974 newspaper clipping published after the bombing reports twenty-three deaths, though the final toll was thirty-three. Fifteen of the deaths were women and two were baby boys. In the clipping, an eyewitness gives this chilling account of what he saw when the bombs went off: "A newspaper stand was blown into the air past me and the newsboy next to it just disappeared in front of my eyes."[14]

While most of us don't have bombs erupting in our streets, the violent, out-of-control nature of our fallen human existence creates a comparable spiritual environment. It causes innocence to disappear in front of our eyes. Forces that move out of our control, whether it's something bad that happens in the day or a sudden shift in our brain chemistry and mood, can blindside us when we least expect it.

The Longing for Heaven-in-Others

This destruction compounds when our family, friends, and spiritual family fail in their attempts to encourage us. Though they mean well, people sometimes miss the mark when they try to console others. We shouldn't be surprised. C. S. Lewis' masterpiece on the theological problem of suffering, *The Problem of Pain*, reveals the complexity of suffering.

It's no wonder many of us get it wrong or avoid it all together. At times, Western Christian culture has bred shallowness and a serial avoidance of the messy anguish that we experience. In our churches, instead of the refreshing aroma of Christ, the Man of Sorrows, we sometimes encounter a strange chemical smell of sanitized propriety—a careful keeping up appearances in our fellowship.

This frustrates us. We long for others to understand our suffering and identity with it as deeply as Christ does. We want the love and empathy of heaven to shimmer in the eyes of others. We secretly dream of a world where we really did follow the command of Romans 12:15 to weep with those who weep. Job's friends, even though they were wrong in their theology, were right in their sympathy (Job 2:11–15). For seven days, they sat silent with Job after his loss—an astonishing expression of solidarity and respect for another person's suffering that is unheard of today. They wept with him in a way that shames the modern Christian's fast-food sympathy.

The Stages of Joy—the transcendent Stabs and aches that fill the House of Longing where we meet with God and the Longing for Truth and for the Truth-of-Others—not only strains for heaven beyond this world and points us to our true home, but it also longs for heaven in each other.

It longs for the bride of Christ.

No matter how frustrating our spiritual family can be, we desperately need that togetherness. We must seek it as if our lives depend on it. And we must avoid at all costs the consumer's approach to the church, as if his bride were a car lot where we evaluate our church experiences the way we assess a car before we buy it. That is Yelp Christianity. Before long, we leave our church to find that new-car smell again.

One of the great diseases of the Western church, especially in America, is chronic church hopping and emaciated, skin-deep commitments and relationships. It's our obstinate refusal to treat our devotion to the bride of Christ the way Jesus does, as a wedding covenant, for better or worse, for richer or for poorer, and in sickness and in health. When things get tough, frustrating, stagnant in apparent growth, or boring at our local church, we're gone. While there are indeed a few good reasons to leave a church, many of the ones we use are often *not* one of those few good reasons.

During a difficult time in my life, my dad wrote a letter to me with a timely (and humbling) quote from Thomas á Kempis, paraphrased in contemporary language: "Be not angry that you cannot make others as you wish them to be, since you cannot make yourself as you wish to be."[15]

We might think this to be a twenty-first-century problem, but it is older than we realize. Lewis was certainly aware of our tendency to focus on the flaws of the church with a ruthless, critical spirit. In his masterpiece *The Screwtape Letters*, an older demon advises a younger demon through letters, and the elder devil brings up this very subject:

> One of our great allies at present is the Church itself. Do not misunderstand me. I do not mean the Church as we see her spread but through all time and space and rooted in eternity, terrible as an army with banners. That, I confess, is a spectacle which makes our boldest tempters uneasy. But fortunately it is quite invisible to these humans. All your patient sees is the half-finished, sham Gothic erection on the new building estate. When he goes inside, he sees the local grocer with rather an oily expression on his face bustling up to offer him one shiny little book containing a liturgy which neither of them understands, and one shabby little book containing corrupt texts of a number of religious lyrics, mostly bad, and in very small print.[16]

We see two portraits in this passage: 1) the triumphant church that Christ has labored to build day after day, year after year, for two thousand years since he rose from the dead; and 2) the blemished surface appearance of this same triumphant church as it digs its roots into an unattractive soil—human beings existing in their grubby, imperfect realness day by day. As in all things, the Enemy wants to point our eyes away from the eternal reality of the church and fix them instead on the daily in-your-face reality, even though this temporal facade will someday melt away forever to reveal our true faces.

Indeed, on the surface the church is full of unpolished people who gather in imperfect church buildings and stumble through muddled services. But this mundane, unattractive church is the foundry where Christ does his most precious, time-consuming work, like an artisan working through the night until every muscle in his body is sore. It is the quarry where he tirelessly mines and shapes his living stones for his Father's temple.

The bottom line is this: a fiercely determined, unconditional, I'm-gonna-do-this-whether-I-feel-like-it-or-not kind of commitment to our local church is what really positions us to mature. Christ has intentionally made the Self insufficient so that we need the Other. We are designed for interdependence—a healthy mix of togetherness with others and sweet aloneness with God. We need both the plentitude and the solitude—the grand gatherings of noisy, hugging, unbearable, irresistible humanity, and the pinpoint sweetness of lonely quiet where no one can find us.

As we embrace both, we will see stunning new angles of Jesus that we never could have known otherwise. We become mirrors of Christ for each other. The longer we allow God to baptize us in each other, the more of Jesus we will perceive, even in a room full of ugliness. And the more of Jesus we perceive, the easier it is to put him on. We can imitate him with that childlike simplicity that keeps pretending until the pretending becomes true. We need each other as magnifying glasses—as mirrors of the King until his reflection is bouncing off the walls of our churches, homes, and hearts.

As Lewis writes in *Mere Christianity*, "Men are mirrors, or 'carriers' of Christ to other men. Sometimes unconscious carriers....That is why the Church, the whole body of Christians showing him to one another, is so important. You might say that when two Christians are following Christ together there is not twice as much Christianity as when they are apart, but sixteen times as much."[17]

Yes, Joy leads us out of ourselves on a mission to others. But Joy also leads us out of ourselves for another reason: we desperately *need* others. Whether we like it or not, if this quest into otherworldly Joy will continue, we must abandon any thought of rugged independence. The journey through Joy never stays in solitude for long.

New Year's Day

In U2's third album, *War*, The Edge steps away from his guitar and brings us one of the most haunting piano performances ever heard on rock/pop radio. It's haunting not for its complexity, though, but for its childlike simplicity. Beneath the piano's simple melody, the other instruments—Larry on the drums and Adam on the bass—are doing what they do so well: sprinting forward with driving, inconsolable motion. The frenetic rhythm underneath makes the piano shine with brighter clarity. It plays in its mid to high registers, and its notes echo with a booming reverb and sonorous delay—a cathedral-sized sound that fills the whole stereo field and makes your car or your room feel larger than it is.

It's the sound of amplified isolation. A searing loneliness.

It works perfectly with the song, of course, as Bono sings with yearning about wanting to be with someone who is far away—a very direct, unassuming cry of homesickness, the intense desire for the companionship of another person. While Bono declares his longing outright, the piano sings it.

What makes the song so interesting—and so emotionally powerful—is the contrast between the singing piano, hanging high and lonely like a bird, with the busyness of the band as it sprints forward restlessly. It is an unsettling combination, though the unsettling feels good, full of a disquieted pleasure.

In a similar way, Joy presses us with bittersweet desire—the "enormous bliss"[18] of longing and the "unsatisfied desire which is itself more desirable than any other satisfaction."[19] This combination of a yearning loneliness in the piano and a restlessness in the band intensifies the sense of homesickness—the need to be with someone else. The desire itself is pleasurable to experience, but its sharpness is almost unbearable. This bittersweet longing shines like a spinning lighthouse lamp. It reminds us of the bitter pill we must take: if we are to overcome, we must surrender to the vulnerability of interdependence.

In an essay about U2 and philosopher Paul Ricoeur—as featured in Scott Calhoun's book *Exploring U2*—Jeffrey F. Keuss and Sara Koenig note how U2 has returned to this theme of interdependence often in their career:

As U2 has affirmed throughout its canon, humans are created to be transcendent—in the language of the Christian tradition, made in the image of God—and, as such, find their vocation in returning to the Transcendent and calling out beyond their isolation and imminent failures to work toward a deep and abiding community.

Yet if humans are created for such soaring heights, why the malaise, despair, unresolved sorrow, and lamenting that define human existence? We suggest that both Ricoeur and U2 would say that the definition of an authentic personhood is ultimately not the modern, post-Enlightenment conception of the self as a singular, isolated, self-sufficient, self-sustaining reality; instead, they would say that the best self is one who is there with and for others.[20]

It comes down to a very practical decision: we must find a spiritual family—a local expression of the body of Christ, warts and all—and stick with them and let the iron sharpen the iron when it must. We cannot be lone-wolf Christians. The out-of-control world and our weaknesses will wear us down.

We need each other—and fast.

The Stages of Joy Playlist

9. "Out Of Control" from the album *Boy*. Summary: The out-of-control nature of the world and our weaknesses throws us off-balance. But even when we collapse, we can put on Christ, an act of faith and reason based on the Word, until the pretending becomes true.

10. "New Year's Day" from the album *War*. Summary: Putting on Christ also means interdependence with his bride, the church, and a longing to be with her. This means dedicating ourselves to a local church with a covenantal commitment.

Scripture

"Do not withhold your mercy from me, Lord;
  may your love and faithfulness always protect me.
For troubles without number surround me;
  my sins have overtaken me, and I cannot see.
They are more than the hairs of my head,
  and my heart fails within me.
Be pleased to save me, Lord;
  come quickly, Lord, to help me."
(Psalm 40:11–13 NIV)

Notes for the Quest

Stability isn't a happy accident, as much as I've wanted to believe that in the past. Whether it's the sure architectural design of a building or a healthy marriage, stability and consistency are planned, and they are often supported and held together by a community.

This is why the command from the Word to put on Christ, to pretend until the pretending comes true, and to take action even if we don't feel like it—to know that doing so is not hypocritical but expected of us—is so encouraging. It gives us a specific strategy, an immediate plan that we can each pursue in our personal relationship with God.

But we must never underestimate the out-of-control instability that lies dormant in ourselves. That's why we desperately need each other. The stronger the community we have around us, the more stable we become.

A Prayer for the Journey

Abba Father, I cry out to you to lead me to safe harbor. This out-of-control world is too much. The weaknesses in my imperfect, fallen nature are too much. The chaos of this broken existence can be overwhelming. Hide me beneath the shadow of your wings. And help me to take refuge among your people, for I know that is the practical shelter you've provided. Please heal any wounds in my heart that were caused by the actions of others, especially the roots of bitterness that may be stopping me from seeking refuge in your church. Give me the strength and desire to pursue a more committed, covenantal relationship with Christ's precious bride. Help me to be as dedicated to her as Christ is. In Jesus' name, amen.

More Bible Verses for the Road

Matthew 5:6; Romans 13:14; Romans 12:15; Job 2:11–15

CHAPTER 11

THE MOON WOULDN'T
LEAVE US ALONE

Whom the gods would destroy, they first make mad.
– *Sophocles*, Antigone

Song to cue: "Every Breaking Wave"
from the album *Songs Of Innocence*

The intense longing of Joy must be handled with care. It pulls our hearts against our ribcages like the moon tugs on the ocean. This can be a blessing or a curse. Wrong reactions to the ache of Joy can lead to a certain kind of madness, to addictive, self-destructive cycles. As Lewis writes in *Surprised by Joy*:

Joy (in my sense) has indeed one characteristic, and one only, in common with [Happiness and Pleasure]; the fact that anyone who has experienced it will want it again. Apart from that, and considered only in its quality, it might almost equally well be called a particular kind of unhappiness or grief. But then it is a kind we want. I doubt whether anyone who has tasted it would ever, if both were in his power, exchange it for all the pleasures in the world. But then Joy is never in our power and pleasure often is.[1]

We try to recapture the blissful ache of Joy after it leaves us. But when we can't exert perfect control over it, we turn to what we can control: pleasure, creature comforts, and coping mechanisms. We settle for second best. Those pleasures, whether vices or virtues, have a dangerous side to them: they become our masters. Suddenly we're sucked into a cycle of enslaved addiction. At a certain point, the addiction stops feeling like a pleasure. It becomes a necessity for feeling normal. Deep down we loathe it. We feel as if we are losing our minds.

But there is hope. And it begins with a journey back in time to the Middle Ages.

Lunatics and the Lunar Eclipse: The Moon's Medieval Madness

Thanks to the moonlit oceans of honeymoon resorts, Beethoven sonatas, Van Morrison songs, and a thousand movie scenes, the modern world associates the moon with love and fiery romance. But long ago in medieval times, the world associated the moon with madness. (This is why the word "lunacy" and "lunar" are similar.)

C. S. Lewis knew all about this, of course. His work on medieval and Renaissance literature is still required reading for university students today. As this note in *Oxford Bibliographies* about English poetry makes clear, "One of the scholarly rituals that anyone interested in understanding the breadth of Renaissance poetry must perform is to read the historical overviews [of] Lewis 1954 and Bush 1945 (the third and fifth volumes of the Oxford History of English Literature) on 16th- and 17th-century verse."[2]

Lewis knew very well how the medieval mind saw the planets, the sun, and the moon. He knew, for example, how they associated Jupiter with kingship and the passing of winter, the sun with gold and dragon-slayers, and Venus with love, creativity, motherhood, and apples.

Interestingly, medieval society associated the moon with all things silvery, watery, and *crazy*. Medieval culture believed that the moon, besides making people lose their minds, produced all the silver on the earth. (And they believed that the sun produced all the gold.) They also associated the moon with water because of how the moon affects the tides of the ocean and the movement of rivers.

C. S. Lewis, knowing all of this, used these motifs to pepper *The Silver Chair* and flavor its atmosphere with medieval moon imagery. In fact, he used this planetary approach with all of the Narnia books.

Scholar Michael Ward was the first to make the remarkable literary discovery that Lewis used the medieval understanding of the Seven Heavens—the sun, the moon, and the five planets closest to earth—to inform the setting, events, and atmosphere of each of the seven Narnia books, as follows: *The Magician's Nephew* (Venus), *The Lion, the Witch and the Wardrobe* (Jupiter), *Prince Caspian* (Mars), *The Horse and His Boy* (Mercury), *The Voyage of the Dawn Treader* (the sun), *The Silver Chair* (the moon), and *The Last Battle* (Saturn). In his book *The Narnia Code: C. S. Lewis and the Secret of the Seven Heavens*, Ward writes this about the story's use of medieval moon imagery—particularly Lewis' focus on water:

> Lewis has the Moon's drenching, drizzling, dewy effects in mind throughout *The Silver Chair*. The theme is introduced at the very start of the story, when we first meet Jill Pole, who is crying on a "damp little path." Eustace joins her, sitting down on "grass [that] was soaking wet." Lewis also describes drops that "dripped off the laurel leaves," that "drip off the leaves," and of "drops of water on the grass." These images, seemingly irrelevant to the plot, are there to help create a definite atmosphere.[3]

Ward then points out Lewis' emphasis on silver and its tie to insanity throughout the story: "The most obvious silver thing in the book is the chair of the title—though there are many other objects, such as Trumpkin's 'silver ear-trumpet,' Rilian's 'silver mail,' and the lamp in Jill's castle room that hangs by 'a silver chain.' The silver chair, where Rilian is tied every night for an hour, is a clear symbol of madness."[4]

The primary lunatic of the story, Prince Rilian, is cursed with a form of madness that makes him forget his identity. The evil witch responsible for the curse has enslaved him. For one hour every night, the curse weakens and he regains his sanity. The witch, however, ties the prince to a silver chair during his one hour of sanity so that he cannot escape.

During his madness, the prince sees everything irrationally.

He stops believing in the sun, and only believes in the moon—that the moon somehow generates its own light. He thinks silver is the most precious metal on earth, and that the evil witch is a benevolent being. As Ward notes about his insanity, "Rilian's mind is the wrong way up. The highest metal he knows is silver, when in fact silver is not the highest or best metal; the highest is gold. But there is no real gold in his world, just the Witch with her 'silver laughs.'"[5]

Prince Rilian isn't alone in this madness. We begin to see things the wrong way up too. When we succumb to the dark side of grief (chronic depression), our perception warps and bends into a dark metal, twisted toward things of despair. We stop believing that the sun exists. We resign ourselves to an endless night.

We begin to lose hope.

And, perhaps most frightening, we begin to *like* seeing things the wrong way up. We become addicted to the old, familiar silvery blueness of our depression.

Every Breaking Wave: When We're Addicted to Tension

In U2's 2014 release, *Songs Of Innocence*, the melodic hook in the chorus of "Every Breaking Wave" is arguably one of the best of the album. Why?

The dissonance.

Usually, dissonance is not something we like. It's what we hear when something is horribly out of tune in a musical performance. As we touched on in chapter 2, we sense dissonance in music when complex, hard-to-decipher harmonic frequency patterns hit our ears and make the brain wince.

But when used in moderation, according to the rules of voice leading, dissonance can turn music into something magical—something that makes people weep at the drop of a hat without knowing why. In the chorus, the big hook of "Every Breaking Wave," U2 hits a powerful note of dissonance at the end of each lyrical phrase. It happens three times in each chorus.

For a fleeting moment, Bono creates what theorists call a major seventh interval above Adam's bass line. The first one happens at 1:12; another one hits at the tail end of 1:16, just as the clock is about to tick into 1:17; and the third one of the chorus lands on 1:20, just as it's ticking over to 1:21. This momentary major seventh clash of Bono's voice over the bass creates a harmonic frequency ratio that's more complex than other parts of the song.

In the brain, this produces a sudden strain of tension. Whether we are consciously aware of it or not, the ear begs to hear the tension resolve. For one full beat, U2 stands tall on the dissonant note. The average band would make the bass player switch notes to follow the singer's melody and avoid the clash, but Adam delays switching notes for a beat until the beginning of the next measure. In that moment of delay, you can hear, at times, Bono's voice bend a little during that note because (I suspect) his brain felt the strain of the dissonance too. But he remains steadfast. He knew he was on to something, and I'm guessing he intentionally wrote the vocal melody that way.

In plain English? The band stabs us in our ears with tension at just the right moment, and then they resolve the tension on the next beat so that our brains feel this quick sense of "aahh" relief. There's a reason why the brain wants to hear the song over and over again. It's addicted to the harmonic tension-relief trigger that U2 pulls throughout the melody.

It's appropriate, considering the song's lyrical meaning. In an interview with *Rolling Stone*, Bono said that the song is about couples who are "addicted to sort of failure and rebirth."[6] We become addicted to the seesaw cycle of insanity and sanity, of binging on earthly pleasures in place of Joy, and then feeling the empty longing that follows, which then leads us to search out more earthly pleasures to fill the void. We form a peculiar codependence on our pattern of failure and restoration. This is often the hardest chain of addiction to sever.

Fortunately, the next Stage of Joy will help us break this cycle. No matter how addicted we are to earthly pleasures, moments of sanity always come, if only for a few seconds. When we come to our senses, when we see the emptiness of our addictions that we've substituted for Joy, a deep longing stirs within us—the Longing for Heaven's Perspective. We long to see from a higher vantage point—from clear air.

Lewis uses this Longing for Heaven's Perspective often in *The Silver Chair*. A huge portion of the story takes place underground or during the night. When the characters go underground, their minds become confused. Lewis creates the setting so effectively that the reader begins to feel claustrophobic—a desperate impulse to get above ground and breathe fresh air again in the sunlight, far away from the moon's madness.

Again, Lewis borrows from the medieval imagination to create this feeling of confused reality and claustrophobia. As Ward notes, "In pre-Copernican astronomy, the Moon marked a major frontier. Above the Moon, everything was believed to be perfect, certain, and permanent. Below the Moon, everything was thought to be subject to doubt, confusion, and change. And it's because the Moon stood at the boundary between those two worlds that Lewis structured *The Silver Chair* the way he did."[7]

In the story, Aslan himself warns the children who have stumbled into Narnia about this boundary: "Here on the mountain, the air is clear and your mind is clear; as you drop down into Narnia, the air will thicken. Take great care that it does not confuse your mind. And the signs which you have learned here will not look at all as you expect them to look, when you meet them there."[8]

Although we are not in Narnia, the same principle applies in this world. There is a higher country, a tall mountain that we must reach. It takes determination and stubborn repetition to reach its summit, but it is crucial to our survival. Like the other Longings in this journey, the moment we feel that Longing for Heaven's Perspective well up inside, we must fix our attention on it. We must go to the places that remind us of that Perspective: to the Bible, and then to people among our families, friends, and spiritual families who know us well and who help us see things from God's point of view.

We can also return to the testimonies of the past—to the memorial stones piled up in our hearts that record all of the good things that God has done. As my mother, a zealous lover of God, penned, "What else could even approximate the majesty and glorious depth of his profound beauty around us, through us, for us?"[9]

As we focus on that profound beauty, we can turn it into a practical exercise and make a list of every good thing that God has ever done in our lives—as much as we can remember. We can keep that list nearby and turn to it whenever the madness of the moon and the subterranean humidity of this world begin to cloud our senses.

Unfortunately, this isn't the only war that we must wage against the moon. There is another kind of madness.

A Second Madness: Dishonest Memories

When C. S. Lewis lost his wife, who went by her middle name Joy, the couple were just three years into their marriage and were luxuriating in the warmth of a fierce new love. Joy was a fitting companion for him. She had an intellect to match his, and she filled his life with a loveliness he had never known. However, after she died, one of his greatest fears in grief was not forgetting her, but remembering a false version of her. As he writes in *A Grief Observed* (which refers to Joy by her first initial, H.):

> I must think more about H. and less about myself....But there's a snag...it is my own mind that selects and groups [the memories]. Already, less than a month after her death, I can feel the slow, insidious beginning of a process that will make the H. I think of into a more and more imaginary woman. Founded on fact, no doubt. I shall put in nothing fictitious (or I hope I shan't). But won't the composition inevitably become more and more my own? The reality is no longer there to check me, to pull me up short, as the real H. so often did, so unexpectedly, by being so thoroughly herself and not me.[10]

It's frustrating to lose a clear vision of someone or something precious in our memory. It muddies things up. It makes the journey through sorrow confusing. Our past begins to feel like a fairy tale. The loss grows sharper. But the most dangerous poison comes when it expands to our relationship with God—when our memories of God's work in our lives are obscured and forgotten or darkened and twisted into something untrue because we can no longer remember the treasures the right way up. When this happens, we lose precious high ground.

The art of remembering, therefore, is both a discipline and a fight.

In Lewis' *Till We Have Faces: A Myth Retold*, we find a heartrending example of this battle—of what it means to have a true vision of someone we love and a clear view of God's goodness toward us. In the novel, Lewis retells the classic Greek myth of Cupid and Psyche. But in his version, the tale is told from the perspective of Psyche's older sister Orual, who lodges a complaint against the gods after she mistakenly ruins the marriage between Cupid and Psyche. The misstep also cuts Orual off from her sister Psyche, which is a devastating loss. Guilt, anger, and grief overrun her. She blames the gods. (And Lewis seems to hint in places that "the gods" in the story are really the Lord God.)

At one point, as Orual mulls over her complaint against the gods, she writes this about the nature of memory: "And now we are coming to that part of my history on which my charge against the gods chiefly rests; and therefore I must try at any cost to write what is wholly true. Yet it is hard to know perfectly what I was thinking while those huge, silent moments went past. By remembering it too often I have blurred the memory itself."[11]

Orual uncovers a problem here: the more we obsess over a memory—and the more we turn it over in our minds—the more the memory blurs or transforms. This tainted memory fills Orual with a complexity of emotions, much of it negative, angry, guilt-ridden. She expects no kindness or mercy, though she presses on to charge the gods with wrongdoing.

When she finally reaches the gods, she learns something astonishing: what she had interpreted and remembered as hostility and judgment from the gods was, all along, an act of mercy. She had been walking in a kind of madness. Not only did she wrongly perceive Psyche, the gods, and her circumstances with a kind of madly obsessed self-centeredness, but she also overestimated her ability to know her own mind. She really did not know herself as well as she thought she did. Her cycle of self-deception became an addiction that ruled her life. In the story, she writes these remarkable words after she discovers the truth:

Often when he was teaching me to write in Greek the Fox would say, "Child, to say the very thing you really mean, the whole of it, nothing more or less or other than what you really mean; that's the whole art and joy of words." A glib saying. When the time comes to you at which you will be forced at last to utter the speech which has lain at the center of your soul for years, which you have, all that time, idiot-like, been saying over and over, you'll not talk about joy of words. I saw well why the gods do not speak to us openly, nor let us answer. Till that word can be dug out of us, why should they hear the babble that we think we mean? How can they meet us face to face till we have faces?[12]

After Orual realizes that she never knew herself in truth— she never had a face, as she put it—the next part of her redemption comes when she meets her little sister Psyche again, whom Orual had been so protective and madly possessive over in the beginning. Orual feels utter shame and falls at Psyche's feet, readying herself for Psyche's anger as she confesses the wickedness in her heart: "'Oh Psyche, oh goddess,' I said. 'Never again will I call you mine; but all there is of me shall be yours. Alas, you know now what it's worth. I never wished you well, never had one selfless thought of you. I was a craver.'"[13]

But Psyche, who is not angry, pleads with her to stand up. At this moment, Orual realizes the falseness of her own memories and expectations and sees Psyche with clear vision:

The air that came from her clothes and limbs and hair was wild and sweet; youth seemed to come into my breast as I breathed it. And yet (this is hard to say) with all this, even because of all this, she was the old Psyche still; a thousand times more her very self than she had been before the Offering. For all that had then but flashed out in a glance or a gesture, all that one meant most when one spoke her name, was now wholly present, not to be gathered up from hints nor in shreds, not some of it in one moment and some in another. Goddess? I had never seen a real woman before....Joy silenced me. And I thought I had now come to the highest, and to the utmost fullness of being which the human soul can contain.[14]

Orual's "utmost fullness of being" can be ours too when we open ourselves to the Holy Spirit's tireless work—especially as he makes use of these Stages of Joy and their branches of Longing. The Longing for Heaven's Perspective not only pulls us to higher ground and saves us from a distorted vision of our circumstances and ourselves, as it did for Prince Rilian, but it also saves us from our distorted view of others, including our loved ones who have passed on.

And we have this hope: when we sit at the highest perch of all, the throne of Christ at the right hand of God—where the apostle Paul says we are seated if we are in Christ (Eph. 2:1–10)—then our confused vision of present circumstances and past memories will clear. Our minds will be the right way up. And we will find that we, for the first time, have faces.

But all of this begs a few practical questions: What else can we do to respond to this Longing for Heaven's Perspective? How do we get to that high perch above the stars and make it a meaningful reality in our daily lives? How do we break away from earth's mad gravity and cross into the clear-headed frontier above the moon?

These will be the questions we answer in the next chapter, and the answers will involve cranking up U2's "Gloria" to eleven.

The Stages of Joy Playlist

11. "Every Breaking Wave" from the album *Songs Of Innocence*. Summary: In the midst of suffering, addiction becomes an easy escape, but it quickly descends into madness. The Longing for Heaven's Perspective can pull us out of that self-obsessed orbit.

Scripture

> "Even though the fig trees have no blossoms,
>   and there are no grapes on the vines;
> even though the olive crop fails,
>   and the fields lie empty and barren;
> even though the flocks die in the fields,
>   and the cattle barns are empty,
> yet I will rejoice in the Lord!
>   I will be joyful in the God of my salvation!
> The Sovereign Lord is my strength!
>   He makes me as surefooted as a deer,
>   able to tread upon the heights."
> (Habakkuk 3:17–19 NLT)

Notes for the Quest

It's interesting how, when we see the world from a high place—the summit of a mountain, the viewing platform of the top of the Empire State Building, or the window of an airliner—that moment can stay in our memory for the rest of our lives.

The view of the world from a high elevation transfixes us. It pushes away all other distractions or cares. In that moment, our entire being is absorbed in the view.

There is a spiritual version of this high elevation, and it is critical that we get to those heights. We need to sense our feet standing on something that towers over all of our problems—that reminds us that those troubles do not have eternal power, and they will not last forever. When we feel our feet on the summit of God's Solid Rock, the truth sinks in: his power and his joy will last forever, but our sorrows will not.

A Prayer for the Journey

Abba Father, thank you for making a way out of the madness in my life and in the world. Help me to walk by faith and not by sight, and guide me up your mountain until I can stand on your heights and see my life from your perspective. Cut off the earthly perspective, the negative vantage point that sees only death, destruction, and evil. Lift my feet off from this ground and place them on the highest summit of heaven. Your kingdom, your Word, and your love remain forever, and nothing can separate me from you because of what Jesus did on the cross. I thank you with all my heart for that grace, Father. In Jesus' name, amen.

More Bible Verses for the Road

Ephesians 2:1–10

The Discipline of Praise and David's Tabernacle: The Most Traditional Form of Worship

> *Therefore by Him let us continually offer the sacrifice of praise to God, that is, the fruit of our lips, giving thanks to His name.*
> – Hebrews 13:15

Songs to cue: "Gloria"
from the album *October*

"Gone"
from the album *Pop*

We walked in the dark through the Ghanian forest, and I had to switch my headlamp off because bugs and moths were swarming to its light and hitting my eyes, nose, and mouth. I was in Africa, deep in the bush near Lake Volta in the country of Ghana, with Dr. Kodjoe Sumney of Mission Africa Incorporated. We traveled with the men of a rural village, visiting the families there, walking from hut to hut, praying with them, and singing songs together. Everywhere we went, we sang.

For a good two hours, as we weaved single file through the forest in almost total darkness, except for the weak beam from a flashlight that someone carried in the front, we repeated a worship song in their native tongue. We sang it when we sat down with the villagers around a fire. We sang it when we got up and left. We sang it when the dark frightened us. Our voices filled the lightless womb of trees around us. And sometimes it felt as if the forest stopped its nocturnal buzzing to listen to our song.

Despite being in the bush on a continent thousands of miles from home, something strangely familiar hung in the air as we sang worship songs that night. It reminded me of my dad and mom when I was growing up, when they would sing old hymns with the congregations they pastored, and, from my seven-year-old vantage point, how the power of their voices shook the air. It reminded me of a bright morning in Poznan, Poland, when Poles and Americans who had just met learned each other's songs, and we rejoiced as if we had known each other our entire lives. It reminded me of my earnest, spiritually hungry church in California and its dogged determination over the years to sing praises to him—as David did before the ark—in both the good times and the bad, even when the roof was leaking and the visitors weren't staying.

In fact, that night of singing in Africa reminded me of *everywhere* I have gone where Christians have been. We are a singing people. And this is not a modern fad that came with the advent of contemporary Christian music. In fact, music goes all the way back to the early church.

When you read the commands of the apostle Paul in his letters to the churches, at first glance, without any other contextual information, you might get the impression that the Christian church in the first century was a non-stop musical. Given Paul's instructions, early church life might have felt like an ongoing flash mob of singing—people spontaneously bursting out in song and singing to each other, face to face, arm in arm, like the film *Enchanted* when everyone in Central Park bursts into a song-and-dance number with Amy Adams's character, Giselle. Meanwhile, Patrick Dempsey's character, Robert, stands bewildered, astonished that dozens of complete strangers are singing and dancing in synchronization, and he says, "He knows the song too? I've never heard this song before!"[1]

Although I'm exaggerating (a little), I suspect that most of us Western Christians would be surprised about how seriously the early church took singing and worship. In his letter to the Ephesians, the apostle Paul tells them to speak "to one another in psalms and hymns and spiritual songs, singing and making melody in your heart to the Lord, giving thanks always for all things to God the Father in the name of our Lord Jesus Christ" (Eph. 5:19–20).

In his letter to the Colossians, he issues the same command: "Let the word of Christ richly dwell within you, with all wisdom teaching and admonishing one another with psalms and hymns and spiritual songs, singing with thankfulness in your hearts to God" (Col. 3:16 NASB). The writer of Hebrews echoes Paul's decree with a similar wording: "Therefore by Him let us continually offer the sacrifice of praise to God, that is, the fruit of our lips, giving thanks to His name" (Heb. 13:15).

The early church, in other words, saw music-based worship and out-loud, thankful declarations of praise as a normal part of Christian togetherness. They saw it as a spiritual offering, an act of the will that they pursued with diligence and discipline, whether they felt like doing it or not.

In the previous chapter, I asked a series of questions: What else can we do to respond to the Longing for Heaven's Perspective? How do we get to that high perch above the stars? How do we break away from earth's mad gravity and cross into the clear-headed frontier above the moon? The answer begins with a simple revelation: we must adopt the Discipline of Praise. We must learn to bring the sacrifice of praise to God every day with the fruit of our lips. Before we explore this revelation further, however, we must take a slight detour to Ireland—to 1981, to be exact.

Stolen Briefcases in October

I do not know Bono personally—at least, not at the time of this writing. However, like most diehard U2 fans, I have, at one time or another, been guilty of projecting my likes and dislikes into the blank space of what I know about him. I assume he's just like me. We do this with all of our favorite public figures. We shape them into mirror images of ourselves. We think, *Wow. Bono's lyrics speak to my life so perfectly, like he's been living in my head. I bet he's exactly like me. We'd probably be great friends if we hung out.*

But reality is less glamorous. I'm sure he and I would share common ground on important things, but like any human being, if I hung out with Bono long enough, I'd find things about him that bugged me. Some of my personality quirks would annoy him too. That's just the reality of being human. And although I'm writing a book about U2's music, that doesn't mean I agree with everything they do or say in public. I'm sure they'd feel the same way about all of us. This book is not a rubber stamp. Neither is it an offering at the altar of U2.

The same goes for C. S. Lewis. A few of Lewis' beliefs and attitudes toward subjects perplex me. He believed in purgatory and praying for the dead, for example, as he states plainly in chapter 2 of *A Grief Observed*. I find that doctrine challenging. On a lighter note, apparently Lewis did not share my taste in entertainment. He felt that Walt Disney's animation, particularly Disney's treatment of the dwarves in *Snow White*, was "vulgar."[2] I like Disney films, even though they are heavily commercialized. (Though, I have to admit, Tolkien's dwarves are much better than the ones in *Snow White*.)

Back to Bono and 1981.

I do not envy the loss of privacy that celebrities experience, especially a megastar like Bono. That constant vulnerability must certainly be one of the shocks of being a public figure. But Bono's challenges with the public began earlier than most, years before U2 appeared on the cover of *Time* magazine as the new sensation of the music industry.

In 1981, Bono's briefcase mysteriously went missing during a tour stop in Portland, Oregon. Somehow it was stolen. It was full of lyrics, private letters, and other personal effects. Thankfully, the case resurfaced twenty-three years later when someone found it in the attic of a home. The lyrics in the case were for the new album that U2 was working on at the time, which would have developed into *War*.

Bono had to rewrite the lyrics for the album from scratch and improvise in the studio, and this changed the band's trajectory. In a May 1, 1983 *Musician* article by Fred Schruers—as posted online by atU2.com—Bono's fierce wrestling match with himself and with the challenges of improvisation in the recording studio are well documented (and, interestingly, Bono misremembers where he lost his briefcase):

The Bono who wrote an entire album [Boy] as an excursion "into the heart of a child" bid goodbye to an emotionally troubled boyhood only to make October by virtually speaking in tongues, raging for days on end into the microphone inside an isolation booth hastily erected of corrugated iron. "Having had my notebook stolen in Seattle a few weeks before, I had no lyrics written down. So I just tried to pull out of myself what was really going on in the songs. The things you are most deeply concerned about, lying there in your subconscious, may come out in tears, or temper, or an act of violence."[3]

Later in the interview, Bono describes the enormous stress of the situation: "I had this feeling of everything waiting on me, and I was just naked, nothing to offer. So I went through this process of wrenching what was inside myself outside of myself."

All of that stress came because of one missing case of lyrics.

The woman who found the briefcase twenty-three years later, Cindy Harris, entrusted it to her coworker Danielle Rhéaume, a scholar, writer, and diehard U2 fan. Rhéaume tells the story of how she got the briefcase—and the fascinating, moving story of meeting Bono when she returned it to him—in Scott Calhoun's engrossing book *Exploring U2: Is This Rock 'n' Roll?: Essays on the Music, Work, and Influence of U2*. (She also reveals details that she found in subsequent research about how the briefcase was stolen in the first place.)

Although the loss of the lyrics caused quite a headache for U2, God used all things for good. As Rhéaume learned from Bono, *October* was fruit that blossomed as a result of the theft. As Bono explained, "What happened was, as a result of losing this notebook, we diverted to October....So, had I not lost [the briefcase], we would have just gone straight into making *War*."[4]

In fact, one of U2's most beloved early songs, "Gloria," emerged from that scramble of lost lyrics and forced improvisation—a song that contains some powerful spiritual metaphors in its musical structure.

Gloria and the Discipline (and Discomfort) of Praise

"Gloria" uses one of the most potent tools in a composer's kit—something that theorist Paul Cooper hints at when he uses terms such as "pitch coils" and "gravity" in his book *Perspectives in Music Theory*.[5] It's so intuitive and brilliant that it's hardly noticeable to the casual listener, yet it serves as the blueprint for the shape of the song from beginning to end.

Before we touch on the song's blueprint, it will help to understand what Cooper means by "pitch coils" and "gravity." Music tends to move toward a fundamental note that lies at the heart of a song's key. For example, if a song is in the key of G, a melody might float around a long series of notes, but when it finally hits a G and when the other instruments play a G chord at the same time, it feels like you've arrived home. There's a sense of tension being released when you hit the key's fundamental note.

Composers know this. They know that the human ear itches for this kind of release in music. And, like any good artist, they use that craving against us. They will take a passage of music and continually dance around the fundamental note, flirting with it and hitting a few near misses where we think the music will finally release the tension.

The longer this takes, the more tension we feel. It builds with urgency. We listen closer. It feels compelling. If we're really listening closely, like someone tracking every second of a symphony as it unfolds, it feels as if we're roaring through the pages of a great novel. The tension builds like the potential energy that's stored when we squeeze a coil. The tighter we squeeze the coil, the bigger the release when we let go. That's why Cooper coins the term "pitch coil."

In pop music, songwriters usually create miniature pitch coils that last a few seconds before hitting the chorus. But in orchestral music, composers have learned to make a pitch coil last for forty minutes of a symphony. In those settings, the pitch coil is so tightly scrunched that the release at the end of the music feels like an explosion. And some composers have gotten so enthusiastic about this release of tension that they hit it over and over again at the end—striking the same note fifteen times as the timpanists beat the tar out of their drums and the orchestra falls out of their chairs from exhaustion.

Pitch coils create a mechanical power in music—an engine of movement. We sense the movement, and after we're done listening, we feel as if we've gone on a journey. It's the same satisfaction we feel when we've gone on a hike and finally reach the end of the trail on the summit. We stop to survey the view and smile with pleasure. We're looking back on the journey below, savoring the arrival. Music does the same thing for our ears.

Of course, composers shouldn't take too much credit for this amazing feature of music. God created the architecture of sound—the overtone series—that contain all of the frequency ratios that make mechanical tension and release possible in music. God *designed* music to have power.

And U2 uses this power well in "Gloria."

For three minutes, it flirts with tension. It keeps returning to the song's chorus where Bono sings in Latin. But each time, the band plays in a subdued key that feels minor and melancholy, not triumphant or glorious. Bono sings with a quiet, hesitant pace. There's irony in it. The song's title suggests something bold and rapturous. Instead, as Bono sings about the struggle of finding words to express his adoration for God (figuratively and literally, since he was trying to record an entire album without pre-written lyrics), we hear uncertainty and shy withdrawal in each chorus.

It's not until 3:25 that the band finally unleashes the melody of the chorus in its full glory—a massive Gregorian chant-inspired deluge of vocal layering sung over major chords set firmly in the fundamental notes of the key. It's a huge release of tension after a three-minute-long pitch coil, and U2 intuitively (or consciously) senses it. The bass, drums, and guitar run with it at full gallop as the cloister of sacred melodies soar above.

The Discipline of Praise follows the same blueprint as "Gloria." There is often a tense struggle involved in establishing a pattern of praise in our lives. Even when we open our lives to a deliberate pattern of worship—when we begin the day with a song of thanks, or when we pause at noon to remember what Christ has done for us, or when we lift a psalm up to heaven as the sun sinks into night, or when we join with our local church and give our best effort to participate during worship songs even when we're not in the mood—it doesn't always lead to epiphanies, grand revelations, or life-changing encounters with God.

It's hard work, and this can create a prolonged spiritual pitch coil. Tension begins to store up. But with each effort, as praise becomes a willful discipline and not a feelings-driven event, eventually the pitch coil will be released. Eventually transformation will take place. Eventually the pattern of praise in our lives will lift us to the high country, and we will have Heaven's Perspective consistently—the bird's eye view that we've been longing for.

And then there is liberation. Performing the act of praise—both praising God and praising the work that God has accomplished in our lives—frees us from a depressed, earthly perspective. If, for example, the precious treasure that we've lost was a relationship—either because the person died or because the relationship came to an end—instead of obsessing over the pain from the loss, we can focus on the good of all that we enjoyed before the loss. We can remember all the things that God did in our relationship and in the life of our loved one. We can remember all of their wonderful qualities that made our hearts rich for a season.

And then we can thank God for all of it—grateful that whatever we did enjoy was allowed to happen, and nothing in the universe can change the fact that it happened. In God's redemptive hands, the good things of the past are indeed set in stone, and that stone will always be there—a memorial statue pointing to God.

In the sweetly saturated, enriched oxygen of gratitude, the past becomes eternally present. We breathe it in once again. It cycles through our hearts and minds, and then it returns to God as we exhale songs of worship and thanksgiving to him. Lewis observes how crucial this Discipline of Praise is in *A Grief Observed* as he contemplates the loss of his wife:

> The notes have been about myself, and about H., and about God. In that order. The order and the proportions exactly what they ought not to have been. And I see that I have nowhere fallen into that mode of thinking about either which we call praising them. Yet that would have been best for me. Praise is the mode of love which always has some element of joy in it. Praise in due order; of Him as the giver, of her as the gift. Don't we in praise somehow enjoy what we praise, however far we are from it? I must do more of this.[6]

Praise, in all the forms listed in the Bible—from King David's dancing and childlike abandon, to Paul and Silas's loud singing in the dungeon—is a discipline, not a feelings-based custom done at our passing leisure. The Discipline of Praise, especially praise that involves our whole being—mind, body, and spirit—is mighty to cast off the cloak of depression and throw the garment of Joy around our shoulders. Coincidentally, this would explain why Paul so strongly emphasizes in two separate letters, using almost identical language, the use of music in our praise and worship.

Music, and the full-bodied participation that goes along with it, pulls in the mind, body, and spirit with a single downbeat. This is partly why a Christian should never look down on another Christian who worships with wild physical abandon—lifting hands, clapping, shouting, kneeling, or dancing with joy—like David did. If we get into the habit of despising Christians who "make a fool of themselves during worship," as we might say, or always questioning their motivations, we should be careful. We might find our hearts turning bitter and barren like the womb of Michal, King David's wife, when she insulted David because he was dancing around the ark of the covenant like a mad man, worshipping God with all of his heart and strength—yes, even all of his physical strength (2 Sam. 6:16–23).

Although this type of expressive worship has been associated with specific denominations and movements in modern Christianity, one could argue that such exuberant, whole-hearted King David-like worship—which was practiced very deliberately, as a disciplined act of the will in David's tabernacle on Mt. Zion (1 Chron. 23 and 25)—is the most traditional form of Christ-centered worship on earth.

Yes, David was Old Testament, but many of David's psalms were prophetic descriptions of the Messiah to come. It was as if the Father had granted David a grace-filled understanding of Christ's work on the cross in advance. This would certainly explain why David would dare worship directly in front of the extremely powerful and dangerous ark of the covenant year-round without being a priest or without following all of the careful rules of Moses' tabernacle. Technically, according to Moses' regulations, everything David did in his tabernacle on Mt. Zion was illegal. But God's grace covered him, and David turned the tent that covered the ark into a twenty-four-hour center for praise and worship.

In the end, the Discipline of Praise, whether it is the wild dancing of David or the quiet kneeling of a Christian in the shadows, is very good at killing the *flesh*, the word that the Bible uses for the proud, fallen nature that humanity has embedded in the walls of its spiritual arteries. It is never very comfortable, and our pride resists it. We like painting over that resistance with a facade of religiosity and purity.

When we come to church depressed or full of brooding ugliness in our spirits, we excuse ourselves from participating in worship. We tell ourselves, *I would be a hypocrite if I lifted my hands and sang while feeling like this*. But then the Discipline of Praise comes alongside us and whispers, "Your worship was never meant to be based on your feelings. Your best day of righteousness is still filthy rags apart from my grace, no matter how you feel inside."

That's good news. That means the righteousness we have through Jesus can also never be tainted by how we feel. This act of faith, this act of will—this sacrifice of praise—is yet another way we can put on Christ. In the Discipline of Praise, we have permission to pretend until the pretending comes true.

In an article about the ancient Hebrew approach to rejoicing in God, Dr. Skip Moen demonstrates how God's way of thinking is so different from modern Western thought. He examines how the Bible uses the word *samah* in Deuteronomy 16:11: "You shall rejoice before the Lord your God" (NASB), and he notes that this word, which is translated into English as "you shall," is an order: "I command you to feel joy." How can God command us to feel? Dr. Moen explains: "In Hebrew, *samah* is an action that elicits a feeling. So God commands us to act in certain ways, and those ways produce the feelings of joy. He commands us to bring the offering, to sing, to clap, to dance, to express gratefulness with mirth and revelry. And what do you know. When I do, I discover I am filled with joy."[7]

That is exactly what happens if we keep worshipping every day and never give up, even when we feel terrible. On Sunday mornings when I feel absolutely lousy, I force my dead-weight hands to lift to the sky. I pry open my jaws that feel bolted shut. I pretend until the pretending comes true. The fog of sadness or emptiness might seem overwhelming, but that vacancy in my spirit will not have the final word.

As my never-give-up mother once reminded me in a note, "Your walk with him is never empty, even when it seems there is a big 'nothing' in your life!" With an act of faith and will, I force my body to participate in worship, even if my heart is not in it. Eventually, like a child imitating an older sibling, my soul begins to imitate what my body is doing by faith.

And then I begin to praise God with real joy, inside and out.

Perched High on Heaven's Front Porch

C. S. Lewis' *The Chronicles of Narnia* began with a simple image in Lewis' mind when he was sixteen, which he then turned into a story when he was forty: he saw a faun carrying parcels and an umbrella through a wood covered with snow.[8] This picture, no doubt, caused a Stab of Longing to prick his spirit when he was sixteen, and his mind kept returning to the image.

The Holy Spirit once pricked my spirit with a similar Stab of Longing—a picture that invaded my imagination. I came across a verse: "Since, then, you have been raised with Christ, set your hearts on things above, where Christ is, seated at the right hand of God. Set your minds on things above, not on earthly things. For you died, and your life is now hidden with Christ in God" (Col. 3:1–3 NIV).

These verses stirred a picture in my imagination. I saw myself sitting on the front porch of a house, but this house was floating high in the stratosphere at night with nothing in view but the glowing earth below and a stratum of stars above. It seemed to be floating in the air like the house from the film *Up*. My feet were hanging over the edge of the front porch, dangling over the earth like a little boy dangling his feet over the ocean as he's sailing on his father's boat. As I pondered the image, it felt as if the Holy Spirit were saying, "You can have this kind of perspective if you build the Discipline of Praise into your life. Don't give up on it."

The whole experience reminded me of one of my favorite moments in Lewis' novel *The Great Divorce*, in which souls in hell (or perhaps more of a precursor holding tank for hell) are allowed to board a bus and visit heaven. The protagonist describes in marvelous imagery his first moments as he enters heaven:

> I got out. The light and coolness that drenched me were like those of summer morning, early morning a minute

or two before the sunrise, only that there was a certain difference. I had the sense of being in a larger space, perhaps even a larger sort of space, than I had ever known before: as if the sky were further off and the extent of the green plain wider that they could be on this little ball of earth. I had got "out" in some sense which made the Solar System itself seem an indoor affair. It gave me a feeling of freedom, but also of exposure.[9]

The first time I read that passage, a deep-cutting Stab of Joy stung in my chest. A similar Stab pierced me the first time I heard the song "Gone" from U2's album *Pop*. The screaming, stratospheric guitar part, played almost entirely in the highest register of the about-to-explode instrument, seemed to sky-rocket even higher into near weightlessness by The Edge's pitch shifter.

The Stab astonished me. I dared not move. A strange wanderlust fell over my mind. The guitar had grabbed me by the collar with both hands and yanked my entire body through the little holes of my headphones until the guitar's hypersonic scream—as beautiful as a siren song—became the only universe I knew. I had gotten out. My mundane day-to-day existence, and the solar system that propelled it, seemed an indoor affair.

These two Stabs of Joy—the reading of *The Great Divorce* and the hearing of "Gone"—had one thing in common: they simulated the hugeness of a Heavenly Perspective that comes to us from the Discipline of Praise. These were little glimmers of the front porch of heaven I saw in my mind—that place where I could sit high above the fray of this world, seated next to Christ, dangling my feet over the world's storms, and safely out of reach. As the psalmist writes, "For in the time of trouble He shall hide me in His pavilion; in the secret place of His tabernacle He shall hide me; He shall set me high upon a rock" (Ps. 27:5).

In other words, when praise becomes a discipline in the midst of grief, the position we have in Christ becomes an experiential truth in our heart of hearts, not just an abstract bullet point in our statement of faith. The Discipline of Praise, if done long enough, creates a permanent groove in our being—a default posture that always tugs at the edges of the sky.

Our eyes become fixed, looking from heaven's perch habitually, always seeing from a perspective that can never be shaken by the earth's tumult. This new vantage point helps us in our pain. But God also uses our pain, with a healthy mix of Joy, to motivate us to make the hike to that new elevation.

The longer we live in this Heavenly Perspective, day in and day out, something marvelous happens: the inconsolable motion mentioned in the beginning of the book—and all of the stages after—converge into a path up the pilgrim's trail, all the way to the final summit.

Inconsolable Praise.

The Stages of Joy Playlist

12. "Gloria" from the album *October*. Summary: The proper way to respond to the Longing for Heaven's Perspective is to pursue the Discipline of Praise. This Discipline, like the act of putting on Christ, is an act of will, not a feelings-based decision.

13. "Gone" from the album *Pop*. Summary: as we succeed in building a Discipline of Praise in our lives, we behold our lives and the world from Heaven's Perspective until that perspective becomes our instinctive, default vantage point every day.

Scripture

"For in the time of trouble
He shall hide me in His pavilion;
In the secret place of His tabernacle
He shall hide me;
He shall set me high upon a rock."
(Ps. 27:5)

Notes for the Quest

The word "pavilion" is comforting to me, somehow. It conjures grandness in my mind, but also seclusion and intimacy. In the context of this psalm, the word's comforting qualities are amplified. It is the thought that God has set aside a secret place—a place where, in the spirit, we can go away and hide in him. Not only that, but this secret pavilion, hidden from the eyes of the world and fallen angels, is set on the highest heights of God's dwelling. Not only do we find refuge and seclusion when we go to him, but we also find Heaven's Perspective. The Discipline of Praise is simply our mode of transportation to that pavilion. Spiritually, it moves us out of the world and into God's secret place in the high hills of heaven. The more the

Discipline of Praise becomes engrained into our daily routine, the easier it becomes to slip into this pavilion anytime we need to, day or night.

A Prayer for the Road

Abba Father, I lay open my daily routine before you, and I ask you to remake my habits and disciplines. Remake the interior of my heart, and turn it into a miniature version of the tabernacle of David, with you at the center, like the ark of the covenant, and praise and worship surrounding you every day, like the priests who worshiped you before the ark in shifts, twenty-four hours a day, 365 days a year. Help me to see praise and worship as a core discipline of my faith, not as a peripheral cultural activity that we treat as a fad of Christian culture. Give me the heart of a committed worshiper who knows the power of praise and knows how to use it. In Jesus' name, amen.

More Bible Verses for the Road

Hebrews 13:15; Ephesians 5:19; Colossians 3:16; 2 Samuel 6:16–23; 1 Chronicles 23 and 25; Colossians 3:1–3; Psalm 27:5

PART V

THERE IS NO END TO LOVE:
FURTHER UP
AND FURTHER IN

WHERE WE ARE ON THE MAP:
A SUMMARY OF PART IV

- The out-of-control nature of the world and our weaknesses throws us off-balance. But even when we collapse, we can put on Christ, an act of faith and reason based on the Word, until the pretending becomes true.

- Putting on Christ also means interdependence with his bride, the church, and a longing to be with her. This means dedicating ourselves to a local church with a covenantal commitment.

- In the midst of suffering, addiction becomes an easy escape, but it quickly descends into madness. The Longing for Heaven's Perspective can pull us out of that self-obsessed orbit.

- The proper way to respond to this Longing for Heaven's Perspective is to pursue the Discipline of Praise. This Discipline, like the act of putting on Christ, is an act of will, not a feelings-based decision.

- As we succeed in building a Discipline of Praise in our lives, we behold our lives and the world from Heaven's Perspective until that perspective becomes our instinctive, default vantage point every day.

CHAPTER 13

ASLAN IN THE DARK: REDISCOVERING GOD

Songs to cue: "Heartland"
from the album *Rattle And Hum*

"Pride (In The Name Of Love)"
from the album *Unforgettable Fire*

The Stages of Joy add up to something breathtaking: an endless cycle of discovering God, and then rediscovering him.

That pattern, "discovering God, and then rediscovering him," could sum up the whole quest. It begins with an unspecified Deep Longing, which develops into a hunger to know God more. When we act on that hunger with determination, he fills us with more of him, just as his Word promises.

But then something curious happens.

After apprehending him and winning the prize, our eyes sharpen. We gain a clearer view of God just by being closer to him. We've reached a higher plateau, and now we see further. We see new angles, and we gasp in awe: there is yet more of God to discover and be had. And that "yet more" is so substantial in that momentary field of vision, so visceral in its shocking size—like rounding a corner in the forest and beholding Everest for the first time—that a divine discontent wells up.

Our previous discovery, as great a stride as it was in our intimacy with him, changes in scale, and what felt like a giant leap now feels like a baby's first step. This stirs a new hunger, stronger than the first, and we rise at once to seek God and discover him all over again. This, as before, cycles us through all the Stages of Joy: the planet-sized longing and far-off homesickness and awareness of heaven and interdependence with others, until we make yet another discovery of him—perhaps while in solitude, perhaps with the church, or perhaps a mix of both.

Then, as the last time, a new panorama shows us yet another piece in his heart that we have not yet explored. And now our recent discovery, which again felt so much like a giant's leap, becomes another baby's first step. We never reach the end of him. And though our character and wisdom grow with each new discovery, our hearts never really leave that fresh, unfamiliar ground that marks the beginning of a great journey. Knowing him, by definition, means continual newness and exploration forever.

This atom-splitting, exponentially growing cycle of rediscovery is the definition of Inconsolable Praise. It is the deep-hearted praise for God that can never be quenched. It never stops moving or seeing new angles of the same Person—the Father of Lights, the King of Kings, the Wonderful Counselor.

We see the most vivid example of this in the book of Revelation, in one of its most intriguing scenes:

Before the throne there was a sea of glass, like crystal. And in the midst of the throne, and around the throne, were four living creatures full of eyes in front and in back....And they do not rest day or night, saying:

"Holy, holy, holy,
Lord God Almighty,
Who was and is and is to come!" (Rev. 4:6–8)

This passage shows the heart of Inconsolable Praise. The four living creatures repeat the same declaration of praise day and night forever.

But why?

When I was a child, the book of Revelation was my favorite book in the Bible. I greatly admired its many spectacles of dragons and towering angels. But this picture of the creatures repeating the same thing forever always made the wrong impression on me—at least, not the impression that the text intended. At best, I saw their endless repetition as amazing but something out of reach for me, something I could never do. At worst, I saw their repetition as mechanical and lifelessly liturgical. The image of wooden birds springing out of cuckoo clocks to sing the same song every hour came to mind.

But this couldn't be further from the truth.

Notice two things: 1) the living creatures fly in the midst and about the throne—they are always moving within close proximity to God; and 2) eyes cover their bodies. This means that, as they move, they see from a hundred different angles at once. Therefore, as they move about the throne of God, they are seeing God from hundreds of new vantage points every second. Their repeated declaration of praise, therefore, is not a mindless liturgy. Each declaration is a unique response to a new revelation about God that they have just seen. Their existence is a continual series of discoveries about God, going on forever.

From this we realize something astonishing: the view of God from Heaven's Perspective is not static. It is ever shifting and four-dimensional, at the very least. Inconsolable Praise is always on the move, running to see more, always sprinting toward the horizon, always planting joyous flags in new ground.

Racing Into the Heartland

The Horse and His Boy, the fourth book in *The Chronicles of Narnia*, is one of my favorites of the series. It takes place during the Golden Age of the reign of the four Pevensies. The sadness of leaving Narnia has not yet fallen upon Lucy, Edmond, Susan, and Peter. Each of them is in their prime. Narnia, and the lands around it, are as bright and mysterious as ever. Adventure blooms at every hilltop and desert dune.

I especially love how C. S. Lewis ties the story of *The Horse and His Boy* to the medieval understanding of Mercury, as Michael Ward points out in *Narnia Code*. Urgent speed, like the running of a messenger, was an important medieval trait of Mercury. It's no wonder then that *The Horse and His Boy* spills over with references to swiftness at every page.

Ward points out a few of them: "There is a great sense of urgency throughout the tale. The cry 'Narnia and the North!' is heard repeatedly. Bree gallops for sheer joy....Aravis says, 'There's not a moment to lose' after overhearing Rabadash's plans. Aslan chases them to the Hermit's dwelling, causing Bree to discover that he has 'not really been going as fast—not quite as fast—as he could.'"[1]

Aslan is cloaked in elusive speed throughout the story. It is a great contrast to the way *The Lion, the Witch and the Wardrobe* heralds Aslan's arrival. In the latter, word spreads slowly across the land before he arrives. Anticipation of his appearance builds gradually. He has stationed himself in a camp with his army, and it is not a hurried operation.

In *The Horse and His Boy*, however, he sneaks into the story with wily speed without even being named. In one conversation with Aslan, the protagonist Shasta tries to explain that he had seen several lions running with him during the night. Aslan disagrees, and Shasta responds with surprise:

> "What on earth do you mean? I've just told you there were at least two the first night, and—"
>
> "There was only one: but he was swift of foot."
>
> "How do you know?"
>
> "I was the lion." And as Shasta gaped with open mouth and said nothing, the Voice continued. "I was the lion who forced you to join with Aravis. I was the cat who comforted you among the houses of the dead. I was the lion who drove the jackals from you while you slept. I was the lion who gave the Horses the new strength of fear for the last mile so that you should reach King Lune in time."[2]

Inconsolable Praise is also swift of foot. It can be loud, bold, abandoned, and triumphant like David before the ark, but it can also be sleek, stealthy, and barely seen as it races beneath a moonless night, bearing our burdens in the dark. Like Aslan with Shasta and the horses in the night, it drives us and carries us through the painful, weighty seasons with a quiet swiftness we never could have mustered on our own.

In U2's restless, pensive song "Heartland," we find a musical pantomime of this swiftness. If *The Horse and His Boy*, one of my favorite books, is one of the lesser known chronicles in Lewis' fantasy masterpiece, then "Heartland," an obscure cut from *Rattle And Hum*, is one of my all-time favorite U2 songs. The reason is simple: "Heartland" has one of the most elegant, emotive chord progressions in U2's catalogue. The chords achieve this through quiet swiftness—a restless rapidity of change that moves beneath the soundscape with stealth.

To understand what I mean, it's helpful to know that any key in Western music has seven primary chords—seven little islands of tonality that a musician can wander around in. This creates seven primary directions where the song can go, assuming it stays in the same key. "Heartland," which is in D minor, begins as many U2 songs begin: a steady beat driving through a single minor chord.

What U2 does from there is interesting. They move like a stealthy speedboat around most of the seven islands of the song's key. They never spend too much time in each tonality. They change the chords at a quiet, restless pace. For this reason, each section of the song feels like a different place in the key. This just adds to the sense of an ever-shifting, subtle swiftness in the music.

New Frontiers Before Us Forever

Earlier in the book, we looked with dismay at Lewis' apparent loss of faith in A Grief Observed, though I would describe it more as a storm of emotions, perhaps, that overwhelmed his usual allegiance to logic. Or perhaps it was more of a lashing out—an angry, desperate swipe at God in response to the crushing severity of his pain. But, whatever it was, near the end of A Grief Observed, the floodwaters recede. The darkness runs its course. We begin to see land again. Lewis regains the footing of his faith.

One of the turning points in this recovery comes at night. As I poured over Lewis' experience, I couldn't help but think of Shasta's encounter at night with the shadowy Aslan in The Horse and His Boy. Similar to how Shasta realizes that he's been mistaken all along about the true identity of the lions—that it was really just one lion, Aslan, all along—Lewis has his own realization in the night: he has been mistaken all along about death and its overwhelming sense of permanence.

The revelation came not through the abstract vision of his intellect—not primarily, at least—but through the strong meat and aroma of experiential knowledge. He stumbled unknowingly into the new frontiers where Inconsolable Praise roams free and wild and always sees God's throne from new angles. With death, what he thought was a gloomy, incomprehensible dead-end—a wall that would cut him off from the land of the living—was in fact the skirting edges of a new country. Lewis writes this about his experience:

One moment last night can be described in similes; otherwise it won't go into language at all. Imagine a man in total darkness. He thinks he is in a cellar or dungeon. Then there comes a sound. He thinks it might be a sound from far off—waves or wind-blown trees or cattle half a mile away. And if so, it proves he's not in a cellar, but free, in the open air. Or it may be a much smaller sound close at hand—a chuckle of laughter. And if so, there is a friend just beside him in the dark. Either way, a good, good sound. I'm not mad enough to take such an experience as evidence for anything. It is simply the leaping into imaginative activity of an idea which I would always have theoretically admitted—the idea that I, or any mortal at any time, may be utterly mistaken as to the situation he is really in.[3]

Although he doesn't admit this initial experience as any kind of evidence, he returns to it again later in the chapter. And then he elaborates on yet another experience he had: a sudden awareness in his spirit that his wife, though dead in body, is still very much alive in the heavenly dimension—a reality that he had tremendous difficulty perceiving in the earlier chapters. With every step away from the darkness, Lewis also begins to look less at himself. This gives us a clue about what kind of country, what kind of heartland, awaits us as Inconsolable Praise moves us swiftly along to new lines of sight around God's throne.

Eyes Turned Outward (Not Staring Inward)

The power and exponential speed of Inconsolable Praise—the fast-growing spaciousness of it—gives us room to stop thinking about ourselves. Our thoughts become pinned on God, like a newly married, doting bride. And then there comes a by-product. Our thoughts fall from the highest branch of the tree—God—to the next lowest branch: others. In fact, Inconsolable Praise releases fresh waves of agape love in our hearts.

The biblical idea of agape love can be elusive, but C. S. Lewis captures it with his usual clarity. His chapter on Charity in *The Four Loves* uses gardening as an illustration—particularly how agape love creates protective boundaries around the other three human loves (Affection, Friendship, and Romantic Love). In Lewis' words, the garden of human loves "teems with life,"[4] but only if agape love tends to them:

> To say this [that the other three human loves need agape love to remain well-ordered] is not to belittle the natural loves but to indicate where their real glory lies. It is no disparagement to a garden to say that it will not fence and weed itself, nor prune its own fruit trees, nor roll and cut its own lawns. A garden is a good thing but that is not the sort of goodness it has. It will remain a garden, as distinct from a wilderness, only if someone does all these things to it.[5]

Inconsolable Praise works hand-in-hand with agape love. It is the gardener's assistant, also creating protective boundaries within our inner lives and removing the weeds of self-centered obsession. Its radical zeal for gazing on God, for finding new angles around his throne and praising him, wards off the heart's instinct to turn inward, especially during difficult times. As my mother once wrote in a letter, "he is our blessing and all that occurs in our experiences (pleasant or unpleasant) are 'love gifts' through his power in us, because goodness will always evolve from them (in our thinking, perception, circumstances) as he wills."

But if we refuse God's hand in shaping our experiences, he cannot repurpose our sorrows into these "love gifts." Instead, our grief will turn into a wallow of self-pity. Nothing will kill our quest through the Stages of Joy more quickly than a heart turned in on itself. Inconsolable Praise—that endless cycle of outward-focused rediscovery of God—helps prevent that.

In the song "Pride (In The Name Of Love)," we see this truth presented in musical metaphor. The openness of the song's intervals—the phenomenon of spreading notes out across large gaps to create a sense of width and vastness in the stereo field—gives us a glimpse of it.

This effect comes through especially well when the music leaps across perfect intervals—the ones that theorists call an octave, the perfect fifth, and the perfect fourth. The distances between these notes are the musical equivalent of the huge wooden frame of a house that contractors build before adding anything else. It establishes stability and a large support frame, creating very clear, immovable boundaries for the house. Without those boundaries, none of the other smaller features of the house could be added.

As Bono sings the classic chorus of "Pride (In The Name Of Love)," he jumps an octave—a huge leap—from where the verse starts. This gives the song that sense of vastness—of epic frame and scale. (That's why the song does so well in large venues like stadiums.) He also leaps down a perfect fourth after hitting the high note of his octave, which establishes a clear tonal boundary. It is a well-ordered, sprawling song with boundaries, like a vast, beautiful garden.

Likewise, Inconsolable Praise creates a Garden of Eden in our hearts. Not only does it send us running down a path of endless discovery and rediscovery of God, but it also keeps our inner lives ordered and beautiful. During times of great suffering in life, that kind of inner order and beauty is worth more than gold. Such treasure allows us to grieve with hope (1 Thess. 4:13).

It allows profound Joy to coexist with profound sorrow.

The Stages of Joy Playlist

14. "Heartland" from the album *Rattle And Hum*. Summary: the Discipline of Praise eventually turns into Inconsolable Praise, and this leads us down a glorious cycle of discovery and rediscovery of God with a hungry swiftness that never stops exploring.
15. "Pride (In The Name Of Love)" from the album *Unforgettable Fire*. Summary: besides sending us on an infinite exploration of God's heart, Inconsolable Praise orders our inner lives and protects us from becoming self-centered.

Scripture

"But we all, with unveiled face, beholding as in a mirror the glory of the Lord, are being transformed into the same image from glory to glory, just as from the Lord, the Spirit" (2 Cor. 3:18 NASB).

Notes for the Quest

When the permanent posture of our heart is Inconsolable Praise, the earth is no longer our home, and the anchor of our souls no longer rests in our circumstances. This not only changes our perspective of the world and our lives, but also transforms our character. It transforms our personality. It transforms the way we live, think, and feel. It changes us on a fundamental level. The Scripture is clear: just the simple state of being near to God and beholding him is enough to transform us from the inside out, "from glory to glory," forever. It is far more powerful and lasting than any therapy or self-help program.

A Prayer for the Journey

Abba Father, please establish Inconsolable Praise in my life. Work in my heart until everything in my life is prioritized and organized around that Inconsolable Praise. Never let my adoration of you become peripheral or some extracurricular activity that I treat as an add-on to all my earthly pursuits. I long for my relationship with you to be the most important treasure of my life. Please use the grief and adversity in my life toward this end—that all the bad things will be repurposed into tools in your hands that bring me deeper into your Joy and deeper into your heart. In Jesus' name, amen.

More Bible Verses for the Road

Revelation 4:6–8; Isaiah 6:1–7; Psalm 139

THE DAWN YOU THOUGHT
WOULD NEVER COME

> His face flushed with a new light...now suddenly the full
> chorus was poured from every branch; cocks were crow-
> ing, there was music of hounds, and horns; above all this
> ten thousand tongues of men and woodland angels and the
> wood itself sang. "It comes, it comes!" they sang. "Sleep-
> ers awake! It comes, it comes, it comes." One dreadful
> glance over my shoulder I essayed—not long enough to see
> (or did I see?) the rim of the sunrise that shoots Time dead
> with golden arrows and puts to flight all phantasmal shapes.[1]
> – C. S. Lewis, The Great Divorce

I had gone to my favorite place on earth: a little marine out-
post of sea bluff trails overlooking the Pacific Ocean. It was
a bright morning on September 9, 2014, when I stood on the
sea cliff, scanning the panorama of roaring, gleaming blue in
front of me. In the morning sunshine, I squinted so tightly that
I could barely look at the world. Gusts of offshore wind leaped
from the Pacific swells below and blasted my face. The events of
the morning ran through my mind again.

I had just finished an interview with Rachel Hendrix, one of the stars in the film *The Perfect Wave*—a movie filled with oceans and sunshine, like the world around me. The movie tells the miraculous true story of Ian McCormack, who died on a surfing trip, saw Jesus, and then came back to life in a morgue.

My conversation with Rachel had provoked a longing to see the ocean, especially when she described some of the photographs that she took during the shoot: "I have a really great shot of [Scott Mortensen] standing in Uluwatu, Bali, about to go for the surf, and he's just looking up at the sky smiling."[2] The thought of someone standing in front of the sea and spontaneously smiling at the sky moved me, and the idea kept running through my mind as I walked on the sea cliff trails.

While stomping happily around the knolls of the bluffs, I received some astonishing news: U2 had just shocked the music world by releasing their new album without warning. Not only that, but they had released it for free to all 500 million users of iTunes.[3]

Even with that news, which came to me through an excited text from my brother Evan, I was slow to catch on. *Wait a minute*, I thought. *I have iTunes.* Crickets chirped for a moment as my brain's computer did the math. "Wait a minute!" I said aloud. "That means I have U2's new album on my phone right now! I have been carrying it around with me all morning without even realizing it!"

For the next two hours, on that sunshine-blasted day at the beach near Santa Barbara, California—with nothing but clear skies, pelicans skimming the ocean's face, and the smell of iceplants and coastal sage—I listened to U2's masterpiece *Songs Of Innocence.*

Although this might make some U2 fans scratch their heads, the third track on that album, "California (There Is No End To Love)," has officially become my all-time favorite U2 song. There are personal biases involved, of course—the song mentions Santa Barbara—but there's also a golden magic to it that I haven't been able to shake since the day I first heard it. It's become a force of nature.

I never get tired of viewing California sunsets—gold so bright in the sky that it stings your eyes—and I never get tired of listening to "California (There Is No End To Love)." In the lyrics, Bono sings about the idea that there is no end to love, and that he knows this because there is no end to grief. He (along with The Edge, who co-wrote the lyrics) observes a profound truth: grief is evidence of love. Grief can't exist if love for someone or something precious didn't precede it. We suffer because we loved first. One is direct evidence of the other. In this way, grief can be comforting. It reminds us of all the treasures that God has sneaked into our hearts when we weren't looking.

What we find in the Stages of Joy is something supernatural: In Christ, it is possible for tremendous Joy to coexist with excruciating sorrow. The world's normal mode of thinking cannot comprehend this. In the world, it's either one or the other. Either we're happy because things are going right or sad because things are going wrong. But in the Holy Spirit, as he expands our lung capacity, we can mourn with incredible intensity while also walking waist-deep through Joy. In him, Joy and sorrow can coexist and form an otherworldly alliance that conspires to birth Inconsolable Praise in our lives.

Joy does not remove grief, in other words; it builds a home inside it and transforms and repurposes it.

It turns us into runners who look, with wide-eyed alertness, toward the finish line. As in the passage from *The Great Divorce*, with each step we're drawing closer to "the rim of the sunrise that shoots Time dead with golden arrows"—to the sunshine that "puts to flight all phantasmal shapes."[4]

The Dawn advances faithfully toward us, just as we press hard toward it. The Joy is only there to make sure we keep our appointment with that Eucatastrophe—the flash that finally makes us as solid and permanent as heaven. It's barreling toward us even now. And though we will discover and rediscover God along the way, the journey is not a circular track that spins on a two-dimensional plane around the same circle forever. It is a three-dimensional helix, a spiral staircase that swings out wider with every turn.

And as each new turn begins, we start over with the Stages of Joy. The Deep Longing returns with its far-off, panoramic, and unspecified desire for God, a new divine discontent fills us, and we're off again on another quest. Yes, grief in this world never ends. But neither does our pursuit of God. And the grief, thanks to Joy's intervention, becomes powerful fuel that keeps the pursuit going.

With each new race, more of God's overwhelming love blasts us in the face like morning offshore winds and sunshine at the beach. And we can't help but look up and smile at the sky when it does. We go further up and further in, pressing our ear to the chest of the Father, listening to the inconsolable motion of his heartbeat.

The Stages of Joy Playlist

16. "California (There Is No End To Love)" from the album *Songs Of Innocence*. In the Stages of Joy, grief and Joy work together to achieve one last goal: to prepare us for the "Dawn that shoots Time dead" that finally ushers us home to eternity.

Scripture

"'He will wipe away every tear from their eyes; and there will no longer be any death; there will no longer be any mourning, or crying, or pain; the first things have passed away.'…And He who sits on the throne said, 'Behold, I am making all things new.' And He said, 'Write, for these words are faithful and true.' Then He said to me, 'It is done. I am the Alpha and the Omega, the beginning and the end. I will give to the one who thirsts from the spring of the water of life without cost'" (Rev. 21:4–6 NASB).

Notes for the Quest

Although grief will always strike us in some form or another in this fallen world, grief will not always be with us. When we try to make sense of the problem of pain, we often forget or refuse to look along the beam of the Bible—to imagine how the problem would look if the Word's promises came to pass. The Bible promises that one day all grief will come to an end. All suffering will stop, and God will heal the pain that history has known. As Samwise asks Gandalf in *Return of the King*, "Is everything sad going to come untrue?"[5]

C. S. Lewis, if he were sitting there with Samwise instead of Gandalf, would say yes. He would reply, perhaps, with what he wrote in *The Great Divorce*: "That is what mortals misunderstand. They say of some temporal suffering, 'No future bliss can make up for it,' not knowing that heaven, once attained, will work backwards and turn even that agony into a glory."[6]

If all the sadness we have ever known will come untrue someday, if all the suffering of history will be healed, this changes our perspective of the present. As the apostle Paul wrote, "For I consider that the sufferings of this present time are not worthy to be compared with the glory that is to be revealed to us" (Rom. 8:18 NASB).

A Prayer for the Journey

Abba Father, I praise you because I know that no matter what happens in the present, in the end your love will always conquer. I thank you that, someday, not only will the final Dawn shoot Time dead with its golden arrows, but it will shoot Grief dead. No matter how dark this world becomes, our hope in you is never defeated. Open my eyes and heart to always have a clear view of that hope. Thank you for being with me through every stage of my journey, good and bad. I rejoice because your love is better than life itself. In Jesus' name, amen.

More Bible Verses for the Road

Psalm 121; Psalm 84

Appendix A

The Complete Stages of Joy Playlist

1. "Where The Streets Have No Name" from the album *The Joshua Tree*. In grief, Joy changes from temporary Stabs to a Deep Longing, expansive and abiding. This creates an inconsolable motion in our lives that takes us on a quest, if we allow it.

2. "Unknown Caller" from the album *No Line On The Horizon*. The quest begins with a rendezvous with God in the secret place. He uses Deep Longing to draw us into a place of abiding communion with him—the House of Longing.

3. "City Of Blinding Lights" from the album *How To Dismantle An Atomic Bomb*. As we spend time in the House of Longing, heaven invades, and we fix our attention on the true reality that lies beyond the blinding lights of this world.

4. "Window In The Skies" from U2's sessions with Rick Rubin and the album *U218 Singles*. As our understanding and awareness of the reality of heaven grows, we experience a satisfying sense of God's divine accumulation of our lives.

5. "Beautiful Day" from the album *All That You Can't Leave Behind*. The House of Longing comforts us with an awareness of heaven, but it is also in motion; it keeps us in transit and uproots our hearts from the comforts of this world.

6. "Zooropa" from the album *Zooropa*. Our digital age threatens to numb our hearts, stop our journey through Joy, and poison

how we grieve. To overcome it, we must allow Christ's rule to create boundaries in our lives.

7. "If God Will Send His Angels" from the album *Pop*. The secular age has disenchanted us and severed God's grandeur from the world. The contrary motion of prayer reconnects what has been severed and preserves Joy.

8. "Ultraviolet (Light My Way)" from the album *Achtung Baby*. Joy leads to a Longing for Truth and for the Truth-of-Others—the hunger and ability to see God's grandeur in the things and people around us.

9. "Out Of Control" from the album *Boy*. The out-of-control nature of the world and our weaknesses throws us off-balance. But even when we collapse, we can put on Christ, an act of faith and reason based on the Word, until the pretending becomes true.

10. "New Year's Day" from the album *War*. Putting on Christ also means interdependence with his bride, the church, and a longing to be with her. This means dedicating ourselves to a local church with a covenantal commitment.

11. "Every Breaking Wave" from the album *Songs Of Innocence*. In the midst of suffering, addiction becomes an easy escape, but it quickly descends into madness. The Longing for Heaven's Perspective can pull us out of that self-obsessed orbit.

12. "Gloria" from the album *October*. The proper way to respond to this Longing for Heaven's Perspective is to pursue the Discipline of Praise. This Discipline, like the act of putting on Christ, is an act of will, not a feelings-based decision.

13. "Gone" from the album *Pop*. As we succeed in building a Discipline of Praise in our lives, we behold our lives and

the world from Heaven's Perspective until that perspective becomes our instinctive, default vantage point every day.

14. "Heartland" from the album *Rattle And Hum*. The Discipline of Praise eventually turns into Inconsolable Praise, and this leads us down a glorious cycle of discovery and rediscovery of God with a hungry swiftness that never stops exploring.

15. "Pride (In The Name Of Love)" from the album *Unforgettable Fire*. Besides sending us on an infinite exploration of God's heart, Inconsolable Praise orders our inner lives and protects us from becoming self-centered.

16. "California (There Is No End To Love)" from the album *Songs Of Innocence*. In the Stages of Joy, grief and Joy work together to achieve one last goal: to prepare us for the "Dawn that shoots Time dead" that finally ushers us home to eternity.

Appendix B

A Look into the Wardrobe That C. S. Lewis Owned and Used for *The Lion, the Witch, and the Wardrobe*

In the early 2010s, while I was employed at Westmont College, I became an informal member of the school's first literary club. This club held a special event at which Dr. Paul Delaney, a beloved English professor at Westmont, gave a presentation about the wardrobe that Westmont has in its keeping. "This is no ordinary wardrobe," he noted. Not only was the wardrobe owned by C. S. Lewis, but it also happened to match the description of the wardrobe found in *The Lion, the Witch and the Wardrobe*, as Dr. Delaney explained that evening in his delightful presentation.

He jokingly teased Wheaton College with a little friendly rivalry when he mentioned that they also own a wardrobe that once belonged to Lewis. But, he pointed out, their wardrobe's appearance does not match the description of the one in C. S. Lewis' book. Their wardrobe has a noticeably ornate appearance, and it has no mirror in the door. Westmont's wardrobe, however—an ordinary looking wardrobe with a mirror in its door, one row of hanging coats, and a second row of hooks attached to the back with more coats—matches the book's description exactly.

For example, when Lucy first enters the room, she sees "one big wardrobe; the sort that has a looking-glass in the door."[1]

When she opens its doors to hide, "she saw several coats hanging up—mostly long fur coats....Soon she went further in and found that there was a second row of coats hanging up behind the first one."[2]

When Lucy's siblings hear her report about the magic wardrobe and go to investigate, this is how the wardrobe is described: "Then everyone looked in and pulled the coats apart; and they all saw—Lucy herself saw—a perfectly ordinary wardrobe. There was no wood and no snow, only the back of the wardrobe, with hooks on it. Peter went in and rapped his knuckles on it to make sure that it was solid."[3]

There you have it: a "perfectly ordinary wardrobe," with a "looking-glass [mirror] in the door," two rows of coats, and the second row is comprised of hooks attached to the back of the wardrobe.

The wardrobe at Westmont College, therefore, is very likely the one that C. S. Lewis had in mind when he was writing the story. That is not to say that the wardrobe at Wheaton College does not have wonderful significance. It was a wardrobe that Lewis had in his family for generations, and he would hide in it when he was a boy and tell adventure stories to his brother and cousins while they hid in it with him.[4] But for the description of the wardrobe in *The Lion, the Witch and the Wardrobe*, it is very clear that he used the one that now resides at Westmont College.

I had the opportunity to visit Westmont College in 2016, and my wife, Amy, took the following pictures of my daughter, Lucy, and me with the wardrobe. (And yes, Lucy also loves the Narnia stories).

The Wardrobe

Q: I've imagined the wardrobe since reading *The Lion the Witch and the Wardrobe* by C.S. Lewis. But how did Westmont get the wardrobe?

A: Dr. Arthur Lynip was leading the England Semester in 1974 and invited Father Walter Hooper, the literary executor of C.S. Lewis' estate to speak to the Westmont group. After his talk Father Hooper mentioned the purchases Wheaton College had made of C.S. Lewis furniture including an heirloom wardrobe and then remarked that, "Of course, there's no such thing as *the original*, but if there were an original for the wardrobe in *The Lion, the Witch, and the Wardrobe* it is still in Lewis's house." Dr. Lynip and some Westmont students went to Oxford and spoke with the new owner of C.S. Lewis's home who was not at all interested in Lewis but did fancy the idea of having American style walk-in closets. The wardrobe had not been sold because Lewis's bedroom had been remodeled in such a way that it would have been impossible to remove the wardrobe without first disassembling it. The new owner sold the wardrobe to the Westmont group for the cost of lumber to build a closet. In the first of the Narnia books, Lewis refers to the wardrobe as "a perfectly ordinary wardrobe, the kind with a looking-glass in the door." The Wheaton wardrobe is ornate and has two doors—neither of which has a looking-glass. Lewis's emphasis that a perfectly ordinary wardrobe was the means of access to the fantastic spiritual realm of Narnia is not without theological significance. We are closer to the realm of the spirit than we some times realize if we are just willing to open the door.

ABOUT THE AUTHOR

 The son of a Bible college professor and a Christian music therapist, Kevin Ott developed his love for theology, literature, and music early in life. After a high school mission trip to Mexico, he also discovered a passion for missions and humanitarian work. These interests led to a B.A. in Music Composition from University of California, Santa Barbara, where he also studied literature and attended summer mission projects with the Christian college ministry CRU. Kevin then joined the worship team of Jubilee Christian Church in Goleta, California, and traveled with them to Europe and Africa to host worship training symposiums. He also became a partner with Mission African Incorporated in Ghana, Africa, where he continues to support humanitarian work and missions.

Kevin is the online editor and a frequent writer for *RockinGodsHouse.com* and the creator of the Aslan's Paw podcast. His writings about music have been noted in a variety of prominent places, from Yale University to the website *atU2.com*, one of the largest U2 fan sites in the world. He has a passion for public speaking, and has given presentations about Christianity, C. S. Lewis, and U2 around the world.

Kevin lives on the Central Coast of California with his wife and daughter, where he serves as a worship leader and occasional guest speaker at his church. He blogs at *StabsOfJoy.com*.

ACKNOWLEDGMENTS

Colleagues, friends, and family members have breathed life into this book at crucial times—either directly or indirectly—and I would not have made it to this point without them. A big thanks to Jim Hart at Hartline Literary for believing in me. To Scott Calhoun, for providing the spark that led me to write about my personal experiences with U2's music, and for being so supportive. To everyone at BroadStreet—Carlton Garborg, David Sluka, Bill Watkins, my editor Christy Distler, Michelle Winger, Natalie Ruffing, Jackie Medina, and everyone else on the team—for your devotion to Christ and your hard work on this project. To the many kind souls in the entertainment or publishing industry who have either aided me directly with this book, opened important doors, or spoken encouraging words at just the right moment (often without realizing it): Randy Phillips, Abbie Stancato, Josh Belcher, Lori Lenz-Heiselman, Dr. Gayle Beebe, Erik Lokkesmoe, John Eldredge, Plumb, Rachel Hendrix, Janet Bozeman, David J. Theroux, Jordan Feliz, Ian McCormack, Moses Sumney, and David Oyelowo.

Endless thanks to my wife, Amy, for your supernatural patience and for believing in Christ's guiding hand at every turn; my daughter, Lucy, for filling my days with more beams of sunlight than I could count while I was writing this; my father, Don Ott, and my brother Evan Ott for reading the book in the early stages and offering feedback (and for your irrepressible humor—laughter is good medicine); my brother Ian Ott for your writing advice in the early years and for sharing your amazing time at Oxford University with me, which pushed me to read C. S. Lewis' nonfiction for the first time; my late mother, Sally Ott, whose writing talent and unstoppable artistic spirit provided a deep inspiration for this book; Devon, Aiden, Keagan, and Emma, for your love and support during this process; Denny and Beth, for your kindness, prayer, and encouragement (and for letting me use your house as a writing retreat); Joy Matthews, for praying for my writing so faithfully; Alyssa and Tyler, for the thought-provoking discussions over the years; my late grandparents, Dan and Roberta Johnston, whose wisdom and generosity made my writing career possible; and to Doug and Louise Ott and the Johnston and Krueger clans for your kindness during the tough years after my mom passed.

To everyone at Jubilee Christian Church. You've been a beloved spiritual family, and you've worked so hard over the years to keep Christ's vineyard preserved. You've kept your eyes looking up toward heaven (Col. 3:1–3) no matter what, even when no one else could see that, and that has meant the world to me. To the folks at Jubilee who joined my email prayer team for this book: Marie Ramirez, Joan Blanco, the many Eymanns (Jon, Julie, Tim, Stacey, Josh, Jonathan, and Tracie), Nick and Cata Galuzevski, Gretchen Gould, Yoli McGlinchey, and Linda Nilsen. To Gérald Pierre for your photography at the media events in Los Angeles. To Eliane Yochum and Westmont College's English department for kindly facilitating my photo shoot with C. S. Lewis' wardrobe. To Troy Harris of Westmont who encouraged my writing early on. To author Carolyn Weber for your encouragement and brilliant example. To Dr. Kodjoe and

Dr. Salome Sumney and my dear friends at Mission Africa Inc. who urged me to write a book long ago. To my friend, Phillip Bailey, for your many edifying words, and to friend and author Lynn Viehl for the enriching correspondence that has been a breath of fresh air.

—Kevin Ott, Valentine's Day 2016

NOTES

(Intro/Always Winter)

1 C. S. Lewis, *The Lion, the Witch and the Wardrobe: The Chronicles of Narnia* (New York: HarperCollins, 2008), Kindle edition, 19.

2 C. S. Lewis, *A Grief Observed* (New York: HarperCollins, 2009), Kindle edition, 49.

3 C. S. Lewis, *The Four Loves* (New York: Houghton Mifflin Harcourt, 1971), Kindle edition, 139.

Chapter 1

1 Matt McGee, *U2 – A Diary*, new updated ed. (London: Music Sales, 2011), Kindle edition, chap. "1986."

2 C. S. Lewis, *Surprised by Joy: The Shape of My Early Life* (New York: Houghton Mifflin Harcourt, 1966), Kindle edition, 21.

3 Ibid., 17.

4 Ibid., 16.

5 Ibid., 17.

6 Ibid.

7 Lewis, *A Grief Observed*, 49.

8 Ibid., 1.

9 John Keats, "Bright Star," John Keats Collection, Work Number 5952, *Bartleby*, accessed October 14, 2014, http://www.bartleby.com/100/383.38 .html.

10 Lewis, *A Grief Observed*, 45.

11 Lewis, *Surprised by Joy*, 17.

Chapter 2

1 C. S. Lewis, *Perelandra: (Space Trilogy, Book Two)* (New York: Harper Collins, Inc., 2012), Kindle edition, chap. 16.

2 *Merriam-Webster*, s.v. "inconsolable," accessed February 4, 2016, http://www.merriam-webster.com/dictionary/inconsolable.

3 Kenneth Partridge, "U2's The Unforgettable Fire at 30, Classic Track-by-Track Album," *Billboard*, accessed December, 8, 2014, http://www.billboard.com/articles/review/album-review/6266759/u2s-the-unforgettable-fire-at-30-classic-track-by-track-album.

4 Marc Graser, "U2 Releases New Album for Free on iTunes," *Variety*, accessed January 18, 2016, http://variety.com/2014/biz/news/free-u2-album-apple-itunes-1201301974/.

5 Paul Morley, "U2 Boy," *Rock's Back Pages*, accessed December, 7, 2014, http://www.rocksbackpages.com/Library/Article/u2-iboyi.

6 Mark Cooper, "U2 a Perspective," *Rock's Back Pages*, accessed December, 7, 2014, http://www.rocksbackpages.com/Library/Article/u2-a-perspective.

7 Sid Smith, "U2 War Review," *BBC*, accessed December, 7, 2014, http://www.bbc.co.uk/music/reviews/3b8c.

8 Partridge, "Unforgettable Fire at 30."

9 Steve Pond, "The Joshua Tree," *Rolling Stone*, accessed December, 8, 2014, http://www.rollingstone.com/music/albumreviews/the-joshua-tree-19870409.

10 Stephen Thomas Erlewine, "Rattle and Hum," *All Music*, accessed December, 8, 2014, http://www.allmusic.com/album/rattle-and-hum-mw0000375268.

11 Elysa Gardner, "Achtung Baby," *Rolling Stone*, accessed December, 8, 2014, http://www.rollingstone.com/music/albumreviews/achtung-baby-19920109.

12 Anthony DeCurtis, "Zooropa," *Rolling Stone*, accessed December, 8, 2014, http://www.rollingstone.com/music/albumreviews/zooropa-19930705

13 Paul du Noyer, "U2 Pop," Pauldunoyer.com, accessed December, 8, 2014, http://www.pauldunoyer.com/pages/journalism/journalism_item.asp?journalismID=359.

14 Brent DeCrescenzo, "All That You Can't Leave Behind," *Pitchfork*, accessed December, 8, 2014, http://pitchfork.com/reviews/albums/8329-all-that-you-cant-leave-behind/.

15 Barry Walsh, "U2 How To Dismantle An Atomic Bomb," *Slant Magazine*, accessed December, 8, 2014, http://www.slantmagazine.com/music/review/u2-how-to-dismantle-an-atomic-bomb.

16 David Fricke, "No Line On The Horizon," *Rolling Stone*, accessed December, 8, 2014, http://www.rollingstone.com/music/albumreviews/no-line-on-the-horizon-20090220.

17 Ibid.

18 David Fricke, "Songs of Innocence," *Rolling Stone*, accessed December, 8, 2014, http://www.rollingstone.com/music/albumreviews/u2-songs-of -innocence-20140911.

19 Henry Yates, "25 Years On U2's The Joshua Tree Still Sounds Incredible," *NME*, accessed December, 7, 2014, http://www.nme.com/blogs/nme-blogs /25-years-on-u2s-the-joshua-tree-still-sounds-incredible.

20 Lisa Grossman, "Why harmony pleases the brain," *New Scientist*, accessed December, 8, 2014, http://www.newscientist.com/article/dn20930-why -harmony-pleases-the-brain.html.

21 "Rock's Hottest Ticket – Time Magazine," U2.com, accessed December, 8, 2014, http://www.u2.com/news/article/5731.

22 Lewis, *A Grief Observed*, 2.

23 C. S. Lewis, *That Hideous Strength: (Space Trilogy, Book Three)* (New York: HarperCollins, 2012), Kindle edition, chap. 13.

24 Lewis, *Surprised by Joy*, 18.

25 Lucinda Borkett-Jones, "Unseen CS Lewis letter on joy discovered in second-hand book," accessed February 3, 2016, http://www.christiantoday.com/article /unseen.cs.lewis.letter.on.joy.discovered.in.secondhand.book/44287.htm.

26 See the complete playlist at the end of the book for a master list of tracks.

Chapter 3

1 Sally Ott, e-mail message to author, January 28, 2001.

2 "Moroccan Riad," *Wikipedia*, accessed December 9, 2014, https://en.wikipedia .org/wiki/Moroccan_riad.

3 Catherine Owens, *No Line on the Horizon*, limited edition magazine for U2's album *No Line On The Horizon* (Santa Monica, CA: Interscope Records, March 2009), B0012638-00.

4 Niall Stokes, *U2: The Stories Behind Every U2 Song*, 4th ed. (London: Carlton Books, 2009), Kindle edition, chap. "No Line on the Horizon."

5 Sol O. Mann, "U2: For Those Who Have Ears to Hear," atU2.com, accessed September 15, 2015, http://www.atu2.com/news/u2-for-those-who -have-ears-to-hear.html.

6 Lewis, *Surprised by Joy*, 17.

7 C. S. Lewis, *The Magician's Nephew: The Chronicles of Narnia* (New York: Harper Collins, Inc., 2008), Kindle edition, 168.

8   Ibid.

9   Ibid., 169.

10 Lewis, *That Hideous Strength*, chap. 15.

11 C. S. Lewis, *The Last Battle: The Chronicles of Narnia* (New York: Harper-Collins, 2008), Kindle edition, 161.

Chapter 4

1   Lewis, *The Last Battle*, 194–195.

2   Lewis, *That Hideous Strength*, chap. 13.

3   Timothy Keller, *The New Heaven and the New Earth* (sermon preached on April 12, 2009 at Redeemer Presbyterian Church), "Timothy Keller Sermons Podcast by Gospel in Life," streaming audio, accessed October 22, 2015, https://itunes.apple.com/us/podcast/timothy-keller-sermons-podcast/id352660924?mt=2.

4   C. S. Lewis, *The Great Divorce* (New York: Harper Collins, Inc., 2009), Kindle edition, 25.

5   Lewis, *The Great Divorce*, 145.

6   Stokes, *U2 (Stories Behind the Songs)*, from chap. "How to Dismantle an Atomic Bomb."

7   C. S. Lewis, *Mere Christianity (C. S. Lewis Signature Classics)* (New York: HarperCollins, 2009), Kindle edition, 136–137.

Chapter 5

1   C. S. Lewis, *The Voyage of the Dawn Treader: The Chronicles of Narnia* (New York: HarperCollins, 2008), Kindle edition, 222–223.

2   Lewis, *The Last Battle*, 194–195.

3   G. K. Chesterton, *The Everlasting Man* (N. P.: Old LandMark Publishing, 2005), Kindle edition, pt. 1, chap. 8.

4   Kevin Ott, "Phillips, Craig & Dean: Interview," *Rocking God's House*, accessed February 3, 2016, http://rockingodshouse.com/phillips-craig-dean-interview/.

5   Lewis, *The Great Divorce*, preface.

Chapter 6

1   A. W. Tozer, *The Pursuit of God* (Harrisburg, PA: Christian Publications, Inc., 2011), Kindle edition, 22.

2 "Out of the Silent Planet," book summary page at CSlewis.com, accessed December 8, 2015, https://www.cslewis.com/us/hardcover/out-of-the-silent-planet/9780684833644.

3 Lewis, *Perelandra*, chap. 3.

4 Ibid.

5 Ibid., chap. 4.

6 "Beautiful Day," *Songfacts*, accessed December, 9, 2015, http://www.songfacts.com/detail.php?id=1039.

7 Ibid.

8 Lewis, *Perelandra*, chap. 3.

Chapter 7

1 Dan Neil, "The 50 Worst Cars of All Time," *Time* magazine, accessed December, 20, 2015, http://content.time.com/time/specials/2007/article/0,28804,1658545_1658533_1658030,00.html.

2 "Zoo TV Tour," *Wikipedia*, accessed December, 20, 2015, https://en.wikipedia.org/w/index.php?title=Zoo_TV_Tour.

3 Edna Gundersen, "U2's 'Zoo': The band lets loose with a high-tech roar," *USA Today*, August 12, 1992.

4 "1,000 Days of Zoo TV, Part One," *Propaganda (U2 Information Service)*, May 1994.

5 "Zoo TV Tour – Tour Dates," *Wikipedia*, accessed December, 20, 2015, https://en.wikipedia.org/wiki/Zoo_TV_Tour#Tour_dates.

6 Diane Scrimgeour, *U2 Show*, (New York: Riverhead Hardcover, 2004), 11–12.

7 James K. A. Smith, *How (Not) to Be Secular: Reading Charles Taylor* (Grand Rapids, MI: William B. Eerdmans Publishing Co., 2014), Kindle edition, 62–63.

8 Ibid., 141.

9 Ibid., 68–69.

10 Ibid., 69.

11 Oscar Villanon, "'The Shallows': Has The Internet Rewired Your Brain?" *NPR*, accessed December, 29, 2015, http://www.npr.org/templates/story/story.php?storyId=127988880.

12 Ibid.

13 Ibid.

14 Robert Osiol, "The Science of Wah Pedals," University of Illinois at Urbana-Champaign physics course 406 resource page, accessed December 30, 2015, https://courses.physics.illinois.edu/phys406/Student_Projects/Spring12/Robert_Osiol_P406_Project_Report_Sp12.pdf.

15 "U2 – Zooropa Guitar Lesson," *YouTube* accessed December 30, 2015, https://www.youtube.com/watch?v=0XRCDOva8UY.

16 "The Screwtape Songs: Bono, C. S. Lewis and Zoo Era U2," *U2 Interference*, accessed December 30, 2015, http://www.u2interference.com/15276-the-screwtape-songs-bono-c-s-lewis-and-zoo-era-u2/.

17 Smith, *How (Not) to Be Secular*, 68–69.

18 Ibid., 141.

19 Lewis, *The Lion, the Witch and the Wardrobe*, 19.

20 Ibid., 163.

21 Joseph B. Bowles, "Moody the Evangelist," *Moody Media*, accessed May 22, 2016, http://www.moodymedia.org/articles/moody-evangelist/.

22 Brian Simmons, *Song of Songs: Divine Romance (The Passion Translation)* (Racine, WI: BroadStreet Publishing Group LLC., 2014), Kindle edition, chap. 2.

Chapter 8

1 "Scientism," *PBS*, accessed February 16, 2016, http://www.pbs.org/faithandreason/gengloss/sciism-body.html.

2 "Petrarch," *Wikipedia*, accessed January 1, 2016, https://en.wikipedia.org/wiki/Petrarch.

3 Hans Boersma, *Heavenly Participation: The Weaving of a Sacramental Tapestry* (Grand Rapids, MI: William B. Eerdmans Publishing Co., 2011), Kindle edition, introduction.

4 *Merriam-Webster*, s.v. "sacrament," accessed January 2, 2016, http://www.merriam-webster.com/dictionary/sacrament.

5 Smith, *How (Not) to Be Secular*, 27.

6 Boersma, *Heavenly Participation*, introduction.

7 Thomas Howard, *Chance or The Dance? A Critique of Modern Secularism* (San Francisco: Ignatius Press, 2011), Kindle edition, chap. 1.

8 Kevin Swanson, *Apostate – The Men Who Destroyed the Christian West* (Elizabeth, CO: Generations with Vision, 2013), Kindle edition, chap. 3.

9 Smith, *How (Not) to Be Secular*, 23–24.

10 Swanson, *Apostate – The Men Who Destroyed the Christian West*, table of contents.

11 Lewis, *That Hideous Strength*, chap. 9.

12 Martin Ryder, "Scientism," *Encyclopedia of Science, Technology, and Ethics, Vol. 4.* ed. Carl Mitcham (Detroit: Thomson & Gale, 2005), 1735–1736.

13 Lewis, *That Hideous Strength*, chap. 13.

14 Boersma, *Heavenly Participation*, preface.

Chapter 9

1 C. S. Lewis, *God in the Dock: Essays on Theology and Ethics*, reprinted in 2001 (Grand Rapids, MI: William B. Eerdmans Publishing Co., 1970), Kindle edition, chap. 6.

2 Ibid.

3 C. S. Lewis, *An Experiment in Criticism* (London: Cambridge University Press, 1961) Kindle edition, 19.

4 Boersma, *Heavenly Participation*, introduction.

Chapter 10

1 Madeleine L'Engle, forward to *A Grief Observed*, by C. S. Lewis (New York: HarperCollins, 2009), Kindle edition.

2 C. S. Lewis, *The Problem of Pain* (New York: HarperCollins, 2009), Kindle edition, 94.

3 Lewis, *A Grief Observed*, 24.

4 Ibid., 27–28.

5 "The Life of C. S. Lewis Timeline," C. S. Lewis Foundation, accessed January 2, 2016, http://www.cslewis.org/resource/chronocsl/.

6 *Time*, s. v. "C. S. Lewis," accessed January 2, 2016, http://content.time.com/time/magazine/0,9263,7601470908,00.html.

7 Sally Ott, e-mail message to author, August 10, 2000.

8 C. S. Lewis, *Mere Christianity (C. S. Lewis Signature Classics)* (New York: HarperCollins, 2009), Kindle edition, 187.

9 Ibid., 187–188.

10 Ibid.

11 Kevin Ott, "Plumb Shares How God Turned Worst Nightmare Into Miracle," *Rocking God's House*, accessed February 25, 2016, http://rockingods house.com/plumb-christian-singer-need-you-now-book-album-2014/.

12 Ibid., 188–189.

13 "1974: Bombs devastate Dublin and Monaghan," *BBC*, accessed January 14, 2016, http://news.bbc.co.uk/onthisday/hi/dates/stories/may/17/newsid _4311000/4311459.stm.

14 Ibid.

15 Thomas a Kempis, *The Imitation of Christ* (Waxkeep Publishing, 2013), Kindle edition, 24.

16 C. S. Lewis, *The Screwtape Letters* (New York: HarperCollins, 2009), Kindle edition, chap. 2.

17 Lewis, *Mere Christianity*, 190.

18 Lewis, *Surprised by Joy*, 16.

19 Ibid., 17.

20 Scott Calhoun, ed., *Exploring U2: Is This Rock 'n' Roll?: Essays on the Music, Work, and Influence of U2* (Lanham: Scarecrow Press, 2012), Kindle edition, 55.

Chapter 11

1 Ibid., 18.

2 *Oxford Bibliographies*, s.v. "English Poetry, James P. Bednarz," under "General Overviews," last modified August 26, 2014, doi: 10.1093/OBO/978 0195399301-0209.

3 Michael Ward, *The Narnia Code: C. S. Lewis and the Secret of the Seven Heavens* (Carol Stream, IL: Tyndale House Publishers, 2010), Kindle edition, chap. 7.

4 Ibid.

5 Ibid.

6 Brian Hiatt, "Trying to Throw Their Arms Around the World," *Rolling Stone*, November 6, 2014, 54–61.

7 Ward, Michael, *The Narnia Code*, chap. 7.

8 C. S. Lewis, *The Silver Chair: The Chronicles of Narnia* (New York: HarperCollins, 2009), Kindle edition, chap. 2.

9 Sally Ott, e-mail message to author, August 10, 2000.

10 C. S. Lewis, *A Grief Observed*, 12.

11 C. S. Lewis, *Till We Have Faces: A Myth Retold* (New York: Houghton Mifflin Harcourt, 1980), Kindle edition, 117.

12 Ibid., 294.

13 Ibid., 306.

14 Ibid.

Chapter 12

1 IMDb's page for *Enchanted*, "Quotes," accessed January 17, 2016, http://www.imdb.com/title/tt0461770/trivia?tab=qt&ref_=tt_trv_qu.

2 Lewis, *Surprised by Joy*, 54–55.

3 Fred Schruers, "U2," atU2.com, accessed January 17, 2016, http://www.atu2.com/news/u2-2.html.

4 Calhoun, ed., *Exploring U2: Is This Rock 'n' Roll?*, 28.

5 Paul Cooper, *Perspectives in Music Theory: an Historical-Analytical Approach* (New York: Harper & Row, 1973) 43–44.

6 Lewis, *A Grief Observed*, 47–48.

7 Skip Moen, "Feeling Commandments," skipmoen.com, modified March 2, 2015, http://skipmoen.com/2015/04/08/.

8 C. S. Lewis, *Of Other Worlds: Essays and Stories* (New York: Houghton Mifflin Harcourt, 2002) Kindle edition, chap. "It All Began with a Picture."

9 Lewis, *The Great Divorce*, 20.

Chapter 13

1 Ibid.

2 C. S. Lewis, *The Horse and His Boy: The Chronicles of Narnia* (New York: HarperCollins, 2008), Kindle edition, 164–165.

3 Lewis, *A Grief Observed*, 49.

4 Lewis, *The Four Loves*, 116–117.

5 Ibid.

Conclusion

1 Lewis, *The Great Divorce*, 145.

2 Kevin Ott, "Rachel Hendrix Talks the Perfect Wave," *Rocking God's House*, accessed February 20, 2016, http://rockingodshouse.com/actor-rachel-hendrix-and-the-perfect-wave-christian-movie/.

3 Marc Graser, "U2 Releases New Album for Free on iTunes," *Variety*, accessed January 18, 2016, http://variety.com/2014/biz/news/free-u2-album-apple-itunes-1201301974/.

4   Lewis, *The Great Divorce*, 145.
5   J. R. R. Tolkien, *The Return of the King: Being the Third Part of the Lord of the Rings* (New York: Houghton Mifflin Harcourt, 2012), Kindle edition, 270.
6   Lewis, *The Great Divorce*, 69.

Appendix B

1   Lewis, *The Lion, the Witch and the Wardrobe*, 6.
2   Ibid., 7.
3   Ibid., 25.
4   "Featured Museum Artifacts," Wheaton.edu, accessed February 21, 2016, http://www.wheaton.edu/wadecenter/Welcome/Museum/Museum-Artifacts.